DESKTOP PUBLISHING

GW00720505

TEACH YOURSELF BOOKS

ACKNOWLEDGEMENTS

Written and edited on an Apple Macintosh™ SE30 2/40 using MacWrite, MacDraw, PageMaker 4™ and MORE™.

With thanks for help and advice to John Flanagan and Nick Clarke, and to Sharon Marshall for her proofreading.

Teach Yourself

DESKTOP PUBLISHING

John Coops

Hodder and Stoughton

A CIP catalogue record for this title is available from the British Library.

ISBN 0 340 55868 7

First published 1991
Second impression 1992

© 1991 John Coops

All rights reserved. No part of this publication may be reproduced or transmitted in any form or by any means, electronic or mechanical, including photocopy, recording, or any information storage and retrieval system, without permission in writing from the publisher or under licence from the Copyright Licensing Agency Limited. Further details of such licences (for reprographic reproduction) may be obtained from the Copyright Licensing Agency Limited, of 90 Tottenham Court Road, London W1P 9HE.

Typeset by Focal Image Ltd.
Printed in Great Britain for the educational publishing division of
Hodder & Stoughton Ltd, Mill Road, Dunton Green, Sevenoaks, Kent by
Clays Ltd, St Ives plc.

CONTENTS

ABOUT THE AUTHOR

John Coops is lecturer in charge of press and radio production at The Media Centre, Blackburn College. He has worked as a journalist in press, radio and television, and as a freelance producer and broadcaster. He took up DTP on Macintosh in 1987 and holds a Master of Science degree in Technology awarded in the same year. He is Managing Director of The Press Bureau Limited, whose work is described in Chapter 11.

1 INTRODUCTION

You

This book is about you. It's about your need to persuade those nearest and dearest to you (your spouse, your bank manager, your accountant, your college lecturer or your DTI adviser) that what you really need before the BMW is a **Desktop Publishing System.** This little book will help you persuade them. More than that, it will equip you with the right questions and observations to cope with computer sales people if you're planning to purchase a computer system. It will help train you to prepare effective documents, and it will help you have fun with technology and be creative. Irresistible, isn't it.

One of the first things to recognise about DTP is that you will taking part in processes with a long history of continuous development which in the past have been performed by people with lengthy training. Commercial art, or graphic design as it became known, has been with us for over a hundred years. Typography and printers have a six hundred year history behind them. You will be eager to find out how to operate the new computer system you are busy unboxing. While you get ready to switch-on, pause for a moment and think about the long and expensive training that designers and printers go through to achieve the results we all take for granted in the pages of newspapers, magazines and brochures. Allow yourself a few moments of humility. Then get a large scrapbook, paste into it pages you admire, and steal their ideas.

Your Audience

Desktop publishing is a serious business. It is part of the route to business success. But to do well in it, you need to consider a lot of factors. You are the biggest factor you've got. Your vision, energy and creativity need to be served well by technology. It's one of the only routes by which your message can reach a big audience. Make no mistake, DTP is a public business. You need to remember one thing above everything else. When you commit yourself to paper, in print, in public, your ideas no longer belong to you. They're in the public arena. Anybody who's got anything to say about the style, content or presentation is absolutely entitled to an opinion. And the audience is always right. However good you think your work is, the acid test is what the audience thinks of it. If everyone is delighted, it's brilliant. If they're unmoved you've got it wrong. However powerful you think your message is, it's the response it rouses in your audience that counts. That's why we say 'communication is in the hands of the receiver'.

If you're going into desktop publishing you need the clearest possible insight into the effects you're having. That means research into your audience. It doesn't take a lot of time or effort to test the effects your products have on your audience. A simple questionnaire or interview survey will do. Test a sample of your audience with a range of styles, contents and presentation approaches. The worst thing you can do is depend on your own taste. You might like a stylish outline *italic script* typeface. That doesn't mean your audience will. Trust what people tell you. Although people answering questionnaires do tend to tell pork pies, you want to be a salesman, and you need to know how to raise hot water pastry.

Whether you want to sell yourself or a product, desktop publishing is a major asset. Use it wisely and well. Step one is to venture into the technology, and devote the time, commitment and cash to developing technical expertise. Step two is to test the products of your publishing skill on their intended audience. If you need help in this, approach your local Further Education College. Many of them are equipped to do surveys for you at a price the professionals would consider insufficient to buy ball point pens. If you've got the cash-flow, hire professional market researchers. Either way, test and test again. People are eager to tell you what they prefer. Bow to their preferences.

Above all else, remember that whatever you intend is incidental. What counts is the message people interpret when they get your materials.

As in television, newspapers, book publishing and gossiping over the garden fence, what counts is the message the audience receives, not the message the transmitter intends.

2 PUBLISHING FROM YOUR DESKTOP

 Features of DTP _____

Time is an essential feature of owning DTP equipment. It can speed up the process of turning thoughts into text and printed layouts. And it can also consume time because you or someone in your business has to learn the processes involved in making a computer do your publishing.

Control is an essential feature of owning DTP equipment. The hardware provides you with control over the way your publishing is performed. And the software provides control over the layout and typography you select.

Seventeen year-olds can produce full colour newspapers using DTP. Estate agents provide their sales leaflets more cost effectively. Bus operators use DTP to lay out all their timetables, leaflets and posters. Companies of all sizes, whose needs include spreading their message cost-effectively, have adopted DTP in their thousands.

Before you decide they must all be right, and go rushing to your corner computer store, you need to decide what you are going to do with your own system. DTP is not cheap to buy or to run. You need to analyse your needs and develop a strategy for use.

 What can DTP do? _____

The brief answer to the question 'What can DTP do?' is 'Every layout and printing job you can think of' – except the highest definition full-colour printing, sizes above A3, and very large print runs.

My favourite restaurant has its menu and wine lists published by DTP. Many advertisements in magazines and newspapers are designed on DTP computers. The newspapers and magazines they appear in are being produced by desktop publishing techniques. Some of the same

 4

computers are even used to design some of the video sequences you see on television. The computer has been applied to publishing very quickly and very effectively. The skills of the printer and publisher are available to the home or business user for a few thousand pounds investment.

The equipment can be used to write a book or design a calling card, print a poster or a party invitation. Most DTP users are involved in two distinct areas.

In businesses and corporations they may publish in-house documents. Their output is likely to be reports, business forms and stationery of many styles and types, perhaps the in-house magazine. In the second area, individuals, small businesses and larger users are involved in designing anything from display advertisements to leaflets and other documents which seek a readership among customers and potential customers.

In the last few years a very large percentage of businesses have taken up desktop publishing in one or another area of their operations. The importance to a new user of analysing their needs and wants cannot be underestimated. Before you spend the money you need to be sure what you want to do with the equipment. First consider some principles.

■ The process itself _____

The process of publishing starts before you switch on your DTP system, and goes on after the leaflets or the press advertisements have gone out. There are four major components in the process which are shown in the diagram overleaf (Figure 2.1).

The diagram suggests that the publishing process is cyclical because what you learn from the results of the last publication, you build into the objectives of the next. We start from the bottom left-hand square. The objectives you want to achieve are defined by what effects you want your audience to experience. Many publishers, for example in newspaper or magazine production, test different versions of a new product on their intended readership.

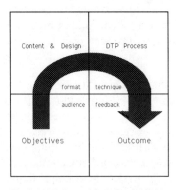

The Four Windows of Desk Top Publishing

Figure 2.1 The Four Windows of Desktop Publishing

Any amount of testing is preferable to none at all. Everyone can fall into the trap of thinking they know who their readers are. The danger is that your image of your audience may be a stereotype. The opposite danger is to assume that you must only provide what your audience expects. Quite the contrary. Effective communication is achieved in direct proportion to the amount of surprise the message causes, as well as it's acceptability.

Once you know clearly what effect you want to create you move into the stage represented by the top left square. The preferred format is the frame within which you design the content and the presentation of your information. Having set your own guidelines, or accepted the company policy, we move into the top right square, the DTP process itself. Here you employ skills and techniques to create the finished publication. The outcome of DTP is not the printed document. It is the effect the document has on (*a*) its audience and thus (*b*) your enterprise. Those results need testing, either formally or informally.

The secret of desktop publishing success is the same as the secret of all communication: 'Know your audience'. And if you don't know now, you'll need to know when you start publishing. In-house, your staff and colleagues will respond to your publications. You'll hear their opinions pretty rapidly. If you're publishing for an external audience there may not be a route for you to hear their views. For assured success you need to create ways in which you can receive feedback.

Feedback is any system which serves to reduce to within acceptable limits the difference between actual and intended performance. Say you set out to produce a handbill and a press advertisement to drum up business for a particular service. It might produce extra business, the same level of business or less business. The feedback could be judged solely on the basis of those results. It's a good handbill/advertisement because business went up. Or, it's a bad handbill/advertisement because business went down. But there might have been an interest-rate hike between you designing the advertisement and its publication. What does that mean for your desktop published handbill/advertisement? It means it might have been brilliant, but external factors affected it badly. The only way to find out is to use your DTP system to design a short questionnaire and send someone out to interview your target audience.

What A DTP System Does

DTP software allows you to make a computer perform page and document layouts. The output can contain text, headlines and subheadings, illustrations, photographs, and other graphical features. A few DTP programs supply all these functions as one package. They are known as 'integrated' programs. In them you create the whole range of the content of your publication. They tend to require large amounts of memory and can be complex to learn. Most DTP packages are 'integrating' programs. You use these DTP programs to import material from other program files stored in the computer hard disk. Word processing documents, graphic images from paint or draw programs, photographs from a scanner software program can all be placed on the pages of your document. It may sound complex, but with a few hours of experimentation, reading the manual and practising, these operations can be performed quickly and accurately.

The outcome is that with the right computer, software and printer you can produce professional-looking documents without leaving your desk.

3 WHAT EQUIPMENT WILL YOU NEED?

A microcomputer for desktop publishing consists of the following items of hardware:

- central processing unit
- hard disk drive
- mouse
- monitor (VDU)
- floppy disk drive(s)
- keyboard
- laser printer

Ancillary equipment could include

- a scanner
- a modem
- a back-up memory device

Figure 3.1 A basic DTP system

The Central Processing Unit

The central processing unit consists of microprocessors which handle information addressing and transfer. They are classified by the terms 8-bit, 16-bit, 24-bit and 32-bit. This figure refers to the processing capacities of the chip. The higher the bit number the higher the speed and memory capabilities of the computer.

Figure 3.2 A CPU

The central processing unit provides two sorts of memory. ROM is Read Only Memory. This memory consists of permanent memory circuits in the ROM chips, which contain information which is not affected by switching off the electricity supply. Many computers hold the operating system of the computer in this sort of circuit. The second sort of memory is RAM – Random Access Memory. This form of memory is available at every work session, but is wiped when you switch off the current to the machine. The more RAM you have available the more work you can do on your computer. This sort of memory requires you to save your work at regular intervals, and this is where the magnetic memory store is required.

The Hard Disk Drive

A computer without a hard disk for magnetic storage is not worth considering if you want to produce DTP documents. As a guide you need a machine with at least 1 megabyte of RAM and a hard disk of at least 20 megabytes capacity to handle the size of file created in DTP software, and allow the software itself to operate successfully.

There are two basically different types of hard disk configurations. Apple Macintosh computers have used the SCSI drive since the early days of the Mac Plus. It is a parallel interface system which transfers eight bits of information at a time. Its strength is that such a device can be used to drive a number of other peripherals, like a printer or a scanner as well as the disk itself. IBM adopted SCSI for its PS/2 models.

Other models use the ESDI standard, in which the data transfer is serial, one binary digit at a time. Typical speeds for ESDI devices are between 10 and 15 million bits per second. Typical SCSI speeds are 32 million bits per second rising to 80 million on the SCSI 2 8-bit standard. In short, SCSI drives are faster and can hold and transfer more information.

The physical components of any hard disk drive work in a similar way. A magnetic platter is spun at very high speed and a read/write head 'flies' across the disk under instruction from the processor to locate particular sectors, each with its own electronic identification code. Clearances are very small indeed, and most units are sealed to prevent particles settling on the disk which could interfere with the passage of the read/write head. When the drive is switched off the read/write head is parked very securely, so such drives can be moved relatively safely while the power is turned off. In general it is recommended not to move hard drives when they are switched on in case a jolt displaces the head.

■ The Mouse

Any computer can work with keyboard instructions, but for ease of use the mouse, which controls the tools on screen in many paint, draw and text-based programmes, is an essential feature of DTP. IBM PCs running under Windows 3 require a mouse, and a Macintosh without a mouse isn't a Macintosh at all, users would agree. You cannot employ paint and draw programmes at all without a mouse, and to change

Figure 3.3 A mouse

tools in a DTP package would be a great deal clumsier without the ability to point and click on screen. If you are to be a desktop publisher you will need to master mouse control techniques.

■ The Monitor

Most computers come with monitor screens which will not show you a full page when you are working at actual size. The smaller Macs have 9" screens, the larger ones 11" screens, and you will need to track across and up and down the page to see your work at actual size. The

Figure 3.4 A monitor

alternative is to purchase an A4 or A3 screen with which to extend your system. Big screens come in three grades; those with 256 greys; those with full greyscale capability (the difference is that photographs on such screen look just like photographs); and those with full colour potential.

There are a large number of such screens on the market at prices which reflect their relative resolutions. As a rough guide the most expensive colour monitor is more than four times the price of a lower definition monochrome monitor. One key feature is the speed of screen redraw, so look for a monitor with a high refresh rate. For almost all DTP purposes you certainly do not need a screen bigger than 19" or 20". The ideal is an A4 (15") screen, or a two-page display (19").

▊ The Floppy Disk Drive ────────────────────

The preferred format these days for floppy disks is the 1.4 Megabyte 3½" disk, which comes in a rigid, protective plastic case. The same size also comes as an 800 Kilobyte double-sided disk. Older versions of the same disk run in 400K single-sided disk drives. In general for

Figure 3.5 A 3½" disk

DTP uses the more floppy storage you have the better, so go for the 1.4M medium. The reason for this is that DTP files with graphics in them can be very memory intensive. Ideally you should off-load all your files from the hard disk to a floppy for storage or archiving. The less you leave on the hard disk the better, since you will need as much memory as possible for running the applications you are using.

■ The Keyboard _____

The keyboard has two distinct uses. At one level it is an electronic typewriter, by means of which you enter the text you will be publishing. At the second it is the source for a series of short-cut commands, or Macros, which you can employ to process the text and graphics, issue programme instructions and even do your filing.

In general, unless you are already skilled in operating an IBM PC or clone, you will find it much easier to produce your documents successfully working with a computer employing a window system. The Apple Macintosh (Mac) or a PC running Windows 3 will give you a screen on which you can enter your instructions much more easily than on other systems. In general its cheaper to buy a PC, but a Mac is more flexible in the range of applications you can use.

Figure 3.6 A Mac keyboard

Figure 3.7 An IBM keyboard

Software You Need To Consider

All computer software can handle print instructions, but that doesn't make them publishing packages. Each operating system requires software developed for it, so what will work on an MSDOS PC will not work on a Mac and vice versa. The most popular software packages which qualify as desktop publishing programmes are:

- PageMaker 4.0 from Aldus UK Ltd (Mac and PC)

- Quark Xpress 3.0 from Computers Unlimited

- Ready, Set, Go! 4.5 from Letraset UK Ltd.

- Ventura Publisher from Xerox (PC and Mac)

PageMaker

This is a popular integrating DTP program. This means that you import into a PageMaker file the text and graphics you need from other programs. The basic processes are easily mastered and a range of facilities you will pick up with practice allow you to produce accurate and professional-looking layouts. In general the lack of sophisticated typographical features compared with some other programmes will not cause problems to any but the most advanced user.

This was the first DTP program, and Aldus have worked hard to ensure that its features are kept up-to-date. It is still the one package you should consider using, and the number of people already using it means you will not be short of advice and assistance. It is priced in the middle band of market prices, unless you want to do process colour separation work, in which case you need to buy an add-on package called Aldus PrePrint which boosts the overall cost.

Working with PageMaker

The heart of PageMaker is the pasteboard on which you specify the required number of pages for the job in hand on a dialogue box which comes on screen when you select <New> under the File menu. Using the <Place> command under the File menu you can locate the titles of the text or graphic files you wish to place on the page. The cursor changes into the text or graphic placing tool, and wherever you click, the graphic or text rolls into place.

By highlighting the text you can specify the size and typeface you want. By clicking on the graphic you can resize it with one of the eight 'handles' which appear on highlighted objects. Items can be pulled off the page onto the pasteboard and dragged back on to another page. You can enter text using the keyboard too, but that's less appropriate than placing it from a word processing package. You can set up stylesheets and glossaries as you work. This helps reduce the amount of time you spend specifying typefaces and sizes. Text can be flowed around objects on the page, leading and paragraph spaces can be altered on the run, and you have kerning control for spacing out large-size type.

Quark Xpress

In its latest form this is probably the definitive integrated document layout package. It has very powerful and precise typographical control, alongside a wide range of built-in features which give a great deal of flexibility over page size and working across multi-pages. Such complexity and precision means the program takes a little longer to learn than many of its competitors, and many users may find they do not need all its features. But if you want to work to the very highest standards of typography it is worth putting in the effort to master Quark Xpress. Cost is upper end of middle band.

Working with Quark Xpress

This involves setting up any number of page defaults using the thumbnail option. These 'master pages' can be edited on the run, but they are there to set the basic style of your pages. You can also set up a graphics library which you access under the Utilities option on the Menu bar. This library contains whatever graphics you choose to enter in it, and items stored there can be towed straight to the page and manipulated for size. Among the built-in features of Xpress are the ability to create drop capitals automatically, vertical justification so that text automatically fills the box you place it in, spell-checking, search and replace commands, fast frame redraw (by specifying greeking for images) and text box rotations in 1,000th of a degree increments. The program is especially strong on colour work, and it is small wonder that so many high-level professionals place great faith in Xpress.

Ready, Set, Go! _____

This was one of the first page-setting programmes, but largescale rewrites made it into a heavyweight contender in the document layout arena. Style features can be set up and cloned across as many pages as are needed using the <Styles> command. Ready Set Go! has all the features of the main DTP packages and is priced towards the bottom of the middle band. It does lack some of the typographical control professional users expect, but it is still worth considering as a relatively cost-effective package.

Working with Ready, Set, Go!

The key concept in this program is 'Draw and Pour'. You specify pre-prepared frames on the page and pour the text and graphics into them. Then you treat the areas by adjusting them to fit precisely on the page. To get text running sequentially you 'chain' the frames by clicking on them in order. In practice this works very much like Ventura Publisher or Quark Xpress.

Ventura Publisher

Ventura was the first document layout programme. Previously page layout had to be handled one page at a time, even if the pages were full of common features. Ventura introduced the idea of stylesheets which meant an operator could set any number of pages to look alike, then fill the layout with text and graphics. That facility created the term 'document processor'. Cost is middle band.

Working with Ventura Publisher

The key to working with Ventura is the Style Editor. Using it involves storing a library of details on page layout preferences, including typesize, placement on the page, graphic areas with or without content; and also detail on paragraph and text styles. You set up the run of pages you're working on, and then pour the text and graphics into these prepared specifications.

In addition there are some other high-powered or specialist programmes which you might require in certain circumstances:

Interleaf Publisher 3.5. from Page Printer Applications plc

This is a complex and powerful integrated technical publishing programme which has word processing, line art, clip art, barcharts text manipulation and page layout all in one package. This program can handle very large publications. Its cost is in the higher band.

Adobe Trueform 2.0 from Letraset UK Ltd

This is a dedicated form production programme, ideal if much of your publishing need is for automated form production. Lower middle price band.

Smartform Designer 1.1 from Claris UK Ltd

A flexible form designer, suitable for a range of forms, charts and tickets. Lower price band.

Multi-Ad Creator 2.0 from Studio Box Ltd

A page make-up programme specifically aimed at producing advertisements with the emphasis on typographical effects. Upper middle price band.

Three low-price DTP packages are also worth a mention. Solo Publisher, Springboard Publisher and Quark Style are among the lowest priced DTP packages on the market.

Solo Publisher from MacSoft

This is a relaunch of an earlier DTP program, and although it has excellent typographical control, it lacks some of the speed and feel of more expensive packages. There is little by way of text editing available, and if you use Solo you must prepare your text in detail in your word processing package first.

Springboard Publisher from Springboard Software

This is slower and less user-friendly than most DTP packages It has good text-editing facilities and strong black and white graphics support, but its page layout capabilities are simple and fairly limited.

Quark Style

This is a 'baby' Quark Xpress which comes with a range of built-in templates to ease the beginner's page layout problems, and it's easy to use. It has limited graphic and typographical features, but might be a good introduction as an entry-level program. It is certainly much cheaper than big brother Xpress.

4 DTP PROCESSES AND SOFTWARE

 Preparing the copy _____

Someone in your office is a fast accurate typist. Using a word processing package needs very little training. The time it takes to prepare text for DTP work can be very large indeed. In general if you are not yourself capable of doing 75 words a minute on your keyboard, find someone who is. There is nothing worse than a two fingered typist to slow down productivity.

Most good word processing packages contain dictionaries and spellcheckers. Some top-end DTP packages have their own built-in. It is strongly recommended that your text should be checked for spelling and typing errors in the word processing package before it is saved and entered into the layout you are working on. There is nothing wrong with checking it one more time on the DTP page. It is simply good practice to check as much of the copy as possible before you do your layout. Subsequent alterations can upset a page or series of pages in the layout phase. And a good spellchecker will also give you a more or less accurate word count on the copy before you enter it, which is always useful in order to fit the copy into the space available.

■ Stylesheets and Your Layout _____

The advent of stylesheets means that you can set up the details of your preferred typefaces, sizes, paragraph formats and so on in advance, and apply a package of style features to each page of a document with the minimum of effort. Setting up a stylesheet or template in advance can save a great deal of repetitive work. The real advantage, though, is that by considering style factors in advance you can apply a purposeful set of decisions in an appropriate and policy-based manner. This means that you are (*a*) going to produce materials with a clear house style running through them and (*b*) you are less likely to produce a spontaneous but unplanned or undisciplined document.

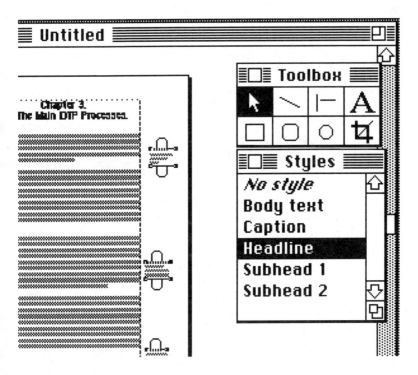

Figure 4.1 This screen dump shows a style edit dialogue box in PageMaker

Stylesheets Are Not Straitjackets

Once your page is up and running, assess the impact of the style features as you set them, and tweak them to fit in their final form. For example the text may be a little short on the page, so increase the leading to make it fill it. Your headline might leave more white space than you expected, so either increase the point size or add some positive kerning to make it fit. The graphic may be contained in too large a graphic area so there's too much white space. Either lower the text repel distance, or stretch the graphic to fit.

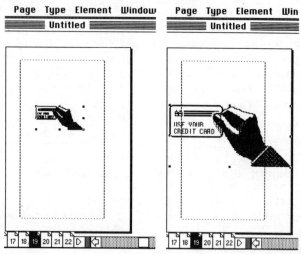

Figure 4.2 This shows the same graphic element before and after stretching

These final adjustments can be the difference between an ordinary layout and an effective one. The stylesheet or the template has already saved you time, and this final tuning would have to be done in any case.

■ Proofing

It is not impossible to proof your work on the screen. If you follow earlier advice you will have proofed the running text in your word processor anyway. But in general you are best advised to run a print of each page, and with a finepoint pen mark-up the errors you wish to correct. Here are a few hints:

● pay particular attention to rules and where they start and finish.

- Check that each page has the same justification, watch out for errors in headlines and other headings since you will very probably have entered these in your DTP programme and they will not have been checked before.

- Watch out for widows and orphans.

Although most DTP packages allow you to correct these easily, many newspaper sub-editors seem not to be able to get rid of these any longer. That's a shame, since the reader is definitely aware of them consciously or unconsciously, and they get in the way of making sense of your story. When the errors are corrected, go through each page with your proofed copy and correct the version on the screen. Do a final Save As and name the file 'Final Version'.

■ Saving and Copying ─────────────────

It is important that whatever DTP programme you use you should save your work at regular intervals. Large documents can place a lot of strain on memory resources. If your work is saved at regular intervals then should the programme 'go down' you will only lose a few minutes' work.

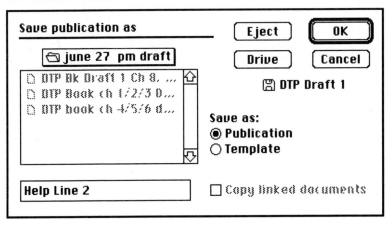

Figure 4.3. The Save As... dialogue box in PageMaker

Key operations at which the risk of loss of your work is greatest are at memory-intensive operations like changing pages or going to the Print instruction. There is no worse feeling than watching a document disappear because you forgot to save before you went to print. Get in the habit of saving before every major instruction you introduce, as well as at regular intervals (say once between every ten and twenty minute interval).

Always keep a back-up copy of your work in case of damage to a floppy disk. Always name your copies clearly, with a relevant title, and note where a version is the final one. There is nothing worse than printing a hefty document, only to find it is the penultimate, and thus unproofed, version. Unless it is not being able to remember what you called the file you are looking for, because the title you gave it doesn't reflect its content or the date it was created.

5 MAKING DTP PRODUCTS WORK

■ Introduction _____

Early page layout programs worked one page at a time. Users objected. They wanted to work on numbers of pages, often with similar elements on each page.

Ventura Publisher, designed to run on IBM PCs, was one of the first programs to provide 'document processing' rather than page layout. In Ventura, users can take advantage of stylesheets and glossaries which allow them to design pages in formats they set themselves. Ventura was instrumental in pushing other DTP software along a similar route towards document processing.

Ready Set Go!, for example gained page navigation facilities between version 2 and version 3, and was immediately bought from Manhattan Graphics by Letraset to replace its own MacPublisher 3. Version 4 of Ready Set Go! boasted a full style editing function, in which words, headlines, paragraph formats and other typographical and graphical layout features could be **tagged** (or saved) by name and recalled with a click on the mouse or a keyboard instruction. Version 4.5 added the ability to specify type more accurately and the package now contains a great number of valuable DTP features. It is especially quick in most of its operations, easy to learn and offers real productivity opportunities to those who need to process long documents with common style elements.

The document processing package Quark Xpress is a fast and powerful DTP program, which in earlier versions had a reputation for being complex. Since version 3 many of the complexities have been simplified and the processes involved have become more intuitive. The program offers the facility to flow both text and graphics automatically across a large number of pages, and has a committed following among print and graphics professionals. It is perhaps too sophisticated for all but the experienced professional publisher.

For even more committed publishers, Interleaf Publisher was the most expensive package for the Macintosh by a factor of four when it was first introduced. It needs a vast amount of memory which it uses in a host of useful automatic and user-directable layout features. Interleaf was a rewrite of the program TPS which runs on mainframes and workstations from IBM, Sun, DEC and Apollo and is probably not the best choice for the beginner.

 ## How to run PageMaker on Macintosh and IBM hardware

PageMaker on the Macintosh and the IBM works in the same way, looks the same, and differs only in minor detail from one machine to the other. You cannot interchange the two sorts of software. IBM and Macintosh software must be kept for the computers they were designed for.

Like all software manufacturers, Aldus are constantly working to update their products. Software updates are signified by number. Version 1 of a programme may be altered and renumbered 1.2., for example. A major change or improvement in the software leads to it being given a new initial number. Pagemaker Version 4 was introduced in 1990. The version 3 series of PageMaker is still in wide use, especially version 3.5. from the late eighties, and it is perfectly adequate for most uses involving laser printing. However version 4 is desirable for its greater control over typography, and its colour abilities if you need them. The one advance most PageMaker users were seeking is also in Version 4, that of being able to rotate text on the page.

Pagemaker is an 'integrating' program. You will soon get used to the routes by which you can import text and graphics into a page layout.

The key for all new users of PageMaker is to remember without struggling. Computer routines become second nature to those curious and bold enough to try things out. Perhaps the one piece of advice you require to be a Macintosh user is 'accept what the computer does'. You are the one who makes the equipment work. The microprocessor awaits your instructions, and with a double click here and a click and pull there you'll find yourself being productive within days.

There are many people who 'click' with PageMaker from day one. They're the ones for whom the computer is not an object of mystery, but simply a tool. They realise they can't break anything as long as they're doing what the machine was designed to do. Training counts here. There are classes for beginners and advanced training courses run by dealers, by freelance trainers and, these days, by local colleges. It is well worth your while to take a short course if only to test out what the hardware and software do. If you're going to pay out hard-earned cash for your own computer it is sensible to try out the equipment first.

Memory

A major point to observe is that any computer you intend to use for publishing will need the correct amount of random access memory (RAM). DOS-based machines will require extra RAM to be installed. Prices for this work fluctuate in line with the availability of components. Macintosh equipment is usually supplied with 2 megabytes of RAM, but four megabyte versions are also common.

Although there are a number of packages which work perfectly happily with 2 megabytes, it is preferable to have access to 4. Running DTP programs with a shortage of RAM slows down every operation, so it is best to have too much! Software normally carries a note of the minimal technical specifications required to run it properly so check that the programs you favour are matched by the RAM of your computer.

Using PageMaker

Perhaps the most fascinating thing about PageMaker on a Macintosh is the number of ways there are to do each operation. One set revolves around 'point and click your mouse'. The second is the keyboard command route, often known as 'short cuts'. See the short cuts section for a list of keyboard commands to speed up your work, not only in Pagemaker, but other software too.

Before you start to use PageMaker you need to be familiar with the operations of a Macintosh. The handbook that comes with the machine gives a detailed account of how to set up, start and use your computer. Assuming you've some basic knowledge of icons, windows, menus and pointers, these are the steps to get your page layout programme up and running on Macintosh.

Switch on your Macintosh. When you sit down to write at the keyboard of a Macintosh computer this is the sort of scene that greets you.

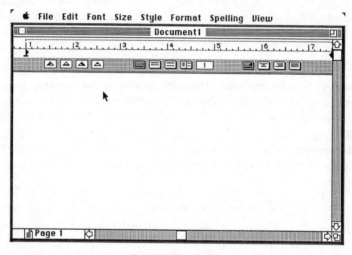

Screen Dump 5.1

On an IBM machine running under MS-DOS your screen will look like screen dump 5.2.

In a word processing program you enter and edit the words for the task in hand. Any job that requires text starts here. People have been known to keyboard text straight onto a page in PageMaker, but that's not really the right way to go about it unless you only have a handful of words to position. Certainly for body text, use MacWrite, or

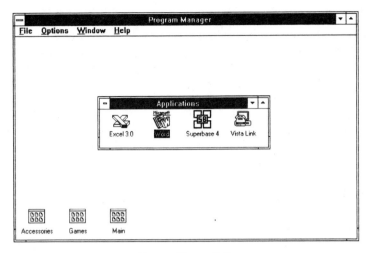

Screen Dump 5.2

whatever word processing package your computer employs, and import it into PageMaker using the 'place' command.

Text

When preparing text for insertion it is best to keep it as plain as possible and to handle all the format issues like text style, font size, headlines and special effects in PageMaker. It may save time to select the right font and typesize before you save the word processor text, but it's not vital. You may be advised, indeed, to save your text in the Unformatted mode, that is as an ASCII file. In general you will not see very much difference in PageMaker between formatted and unformatted text. But in jobs which involve large amounts of text running over a great number of pages you would be best advised to use unformatted text if only to save a little time over a long task.

When your text is finished and checked for spelling, save it by going to Save As... In general it is best to save your work on a floppy disk, and make a second copy to back-up important files. You can save everything to hard disk but you will (*a*) run out of storage memory eventually, and (*b*) cause faster fragmentation of the hard disk.

Fragmentation is a disturbance of the sectors on the magnetic disk which inevitably occurs with a great deal of writing to and deletion from the disk. Its effect is felt gradually and the speed of your computer, and sometimes its accuracy, can be adversely affected. Many experts advise users to de-fragment the disk at regular intervals (say, quarterly). This process involves using specific software to rebuild the sectors on the disk. This takes time, and some programs require you to back-up all your hard disk information onto floppies in order to do the job. So it's in your own interests to keep your work on floppies, not on the hard disk, whenever you can.

Graphics

You may also need to prepare your graphics for addition to your layout. This can be done in a number of ways. You can create your own charts, diagrams and drawings electronically using Draw and Paint programmes. These will often be bit map images saved as PICT (for draw images) or Paint (from paint programs). PICT files differ from paint files in that they are made up from lines and curves which are mathematically defined and can be scaled up or down without disturbing the ratios between the shapes.

With paint images it's better to scale with the shift key held down. This ought to preserve the scale of the original. More sophisticated packages like Freehand, Canvas or Illustrator were designed to work with laserprinters, and they allow you to create files in TIFF or EPS form, which produce unjagged images. In either case, files should be saved for placing into a PageMaker document, probably on the same floppy disk as the text.

You may need to include photographic images in your layout, in which case you will need to scan in the original to create a digital version. This you save as a TIFF file for general use, or as EPSF where you need greyscales and where you have no shortage of memory. A photographic image in TIFF format can quite commonly run as high as 800K. An EPS file at the same dimensions could be as high as 1500K. The latter is too large even for a 1.4M floppy to hold, so software manufacturers offer EPSF Compressed files to alleviate storage problems.

If you do hit storage problems caused by lack of memory, try scaling down the size of the photograph during the scanning process. Even an 86% reduction can produce startling savings in memory.

With your text and images safely stored away, now is the time to double click on the PageMaker Icon on your hard disk, or enter the file code on your PC screen, to access your page layout programme. If it isn't there, insert the floppy disks with the program on them and copy them across.

When you double click on the PageMaker icon you'll see the message box about your version of the program, and a lovely piece of artwork, the Aldus logograph. Then nothing.

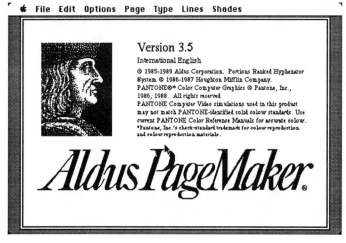

Screen Dump 5.3

At this point people have been known to turn from the screen and complain 'It's stuck', or 'Nothing's happening'. That's because PageMaker is waiting for you. Go to the File menu with the pointer, click and hold and drag down to the entry NEW. Let go when the word NEW is highlighted (that is, reversed, white on black).

You'll get a dialogue box asking you format questions as shown in screen dump 5.4.

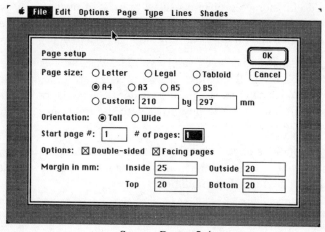

Screen Dump 5.4

You will find it convenient always to work across four pages, usually A4, High, Double-sided and Facing pages. Even if you know the product is to be a single A4 sheet printed both sides, you still may need to set up what might be called 'overflow pages' to make sure your text is where it should be on the finished product. This point will be explained very soon.

Now you've set your pages up, click on OK or hit carriage return (the keyboard shortcut for OK on all Macintosh programmes). The first of your pages will appear on the screen.

You will probably have an idea of what you want your pages to look like. There may be a graphic to go in the centre of the page with text running around it and a headline across the top of the page. You can insert guidelines to help you line up these elements by clicking and holding at the edge of the desktop where the rulers are and pulling across to the page.

These dotted lines do not print and can be disposed of when you've finished with them by reversing the procedure for obtaining them. One hint here. Whenever you seek to locate an item on a Pagemaker screen by pointing and clicking, because every element is 'live' and

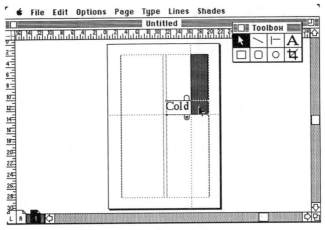

Screen Dump 5.5

moveable, try to click at a point where one element does not touch or overlap another element. You will save yourself a great deal of time and patience by training yourself to do this from day one.

You will find more information on using PageMaker in chapter 9, *Learning Layout Skills*.

6 FORMATS AND THEIR USES IN DTP

There are a very large number of options in publishing, not least in the area of choosing a format. From the sub-page formats of display advertisements, through single page flyers, posters and leaflets to documents like reports, booklets and journals the publisher has choices to make. Whilst most people are well acquainted with the range of formats that printed materials may follow, it may be as well to consider the uses to which each format is put, and the features that your readers will expect to see in each of them.

Flyers, Leaflets and Posters

Each of these is a single page publication. The differences are that a poster is usually much larger than a flyer, and a leaflet is double-sided.

Flyers

These can be handed out in the street and put through people's letterboxes, or commonly slipped inside a free newspaper or under the windscreen wiper of your car. Although this annoys some people, flyers seem to be relatively popular in some business circles.

Leaflets

These are commonly kept on display in places where the population can pick them up if they wish. They can be elaborately designed and printed, and although all consist of a single sheet, it is surprising how much information can be conveyed on, say, a single A4 sheet. The most interesting leaflet effects come with specifying the folds on the page. By folding an A4 leaflet into two vertically or horizontally, or even three horizontally, a multi-page effect can be generated. This interests the reader by making the information seem more complex than perhaps it really is. The folded or multi-folded effect is possibly one reason why some people think of a leaflet as a multi-page document, which of course it isn't.

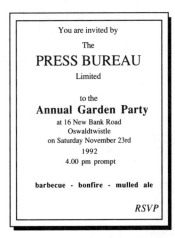

Figure 6.1 An example of a flyer

Posters

These are flyers printed larger, and very similar design features can be found in both formats. Headlines, subheadings and text as well as illustrations are presented simply and clearly in either case. Full-colour eight or sixteen sheet billboard posters are very expensive and elaborate artefacts, but they share features of the simplest 'Our New Premises Are ...' poster. With care and attention to typography and illustration any message can be turned into a poster using multiple A4 sheets or an A3 sheet if you've got an A3 printer or enlarging photocopier. You could create an A3 version to use as a poster and an A5 version to use as a flyer or leaflet from the same piece of artwork. For small runs, or on-demand publishing nothing could be easier. The desktop publisher need never hang up a tatty sheet of lined A4 with a magic marker message on it ever again.

Display advertisements

Display ads in newspapers and magazines are usually designed and laid out by the publication's own designers. Inevitably there is likely to be a house style, and if you provide your advertisements camera ready, like many corporate advertisers do, yours may stand out because of its different style. There is at least one DTP programme specifically for designing display advertisements, but any programme with good typesetting features can be used.

Figure 6.2. This advertisement was designed by a seventeen year old DTP operator

The conventions of display advertisements in terms of boxes, illustrations (for example your company logo), headlines, descriptive and commercial text, typographical treatment and their layout in the given area are all within the capabilities of all DTP packages. It may not be worth your while to do your own artwork unless you value the control over your company's image that creating your own advertisement can give you. It is probably just as time consuming to issue clear and accurate instructions to someone else designing your advertisement as it is to do it yourself.

■ Business Communication _____

Letterheads, standard letters, memos, invoices and receipts_____

Along with any other standard formats you use such as **forms**, all these can all be held on file in your DTP system as templates. By calling them up on screen you can keyboard in the required text and print them out. If your working system requires it you can save each one by day and time, type or client in a relevant folder, or save a hard copy from the laserprinter. By setting up a stylesheet in each template you can ensure that everyone who has to issue such a communication will do it in the same way.

In this area DTP overlaps with the use of a database program. It may be that your database of products, services and clients can generate the necessary paperwork for you, but that you can import into it the DTP documents you have created. An increasing number of database programmes contain DTP elements, and manufacturers are marketing integrated packages. In this context it is best to explain your needs to your software manufacturers or distributors and let them advise you.

Figure 6.3 This graphic was designed and printed on a DTP system

Reports

This is one of the commonest uses for DTP in the corporate world, where more reports are being generated by more people more quickly than at any time in industrial history. By definition a report is an account of a current process or one which is newly completed or about to be launched. It is thus not surprising that the speed with which desktop publishing allows an individual or group to respond has led to an enthusiastic corporate response to the technology.

There are several conventions in report writing, but the most popular is the narrative report, in which headings such as Background, Introduction, Findings, Conclusions and Recommendations are used. Charts and graphs can be imported as tiff files from other software and assembled in the document with cut and paste or draw and pour methods, and any DTP package will enable you to produce effectively presented reports.

In education an increasing number of students are using DTP to present reports, handbooks and even newspapers and magazines as part of their coursework. Any technology which encourages people to marshal and present current information effectively is to be applauded. Wherever speed of response is important DTP can play a positive and decisive role.

Forms

There are specific DTP packages for creating forms. Most mainstream DTP packages will make forms, and surprisingly accurate and complex they can be in the hands of a skilled operator. But there are disadvantages in terms of not being able to lock-in the components in some software. Thus you may in a very complex form inadvertently move an element without noticing until after printing. Specialist form-making programmes like Adobe Trueform or Claris's Smartform Designer can produce excellent results in terms of both ease of use and output quality.

Handbooks and Catalogues

A major advantage you gain with DTP is ease of updating documentation. Handbooks about operating processes or equipment

Contributor's Accounts	**Delivery Note**

According to our records we have supplied you with the following items of news copy, and have not yet been credited for our work.

Title of Story	
Ordered by	
Date of despatch	
Method of despatch	
Length	
Fee	

Figure 6.4 Sample delivery note

can be updated with each technical change. Catalogues can be reprinted as stocks change, if you're running an on-demand publishing system.

Newsletters, Newspapers and Journals

Major projects like these have been the property of highly specialised groups until the advent of DTP. Their successful completion depends on employing the skills of a printing company. DTP technology is being widely adopted in the professional publishing industry, and the work of these professionals will always be significantly better than the output of the multi-purpose desktop publisher for the simple reason that they have access to the very best dedicated printing technology and staff. Having made that claim, it is apparent that expertise in producing newspapers and magazines is spreading with DTP. Small and medium-sized companies, schools and colleges, and small independent publishers are all producing more professional-looking publications as a result of developing DTP skills. Perhaps the over-riding need is for anyone involving themselves in such projects to read at least one of the textbooks on newspaper and magazine layout and production.

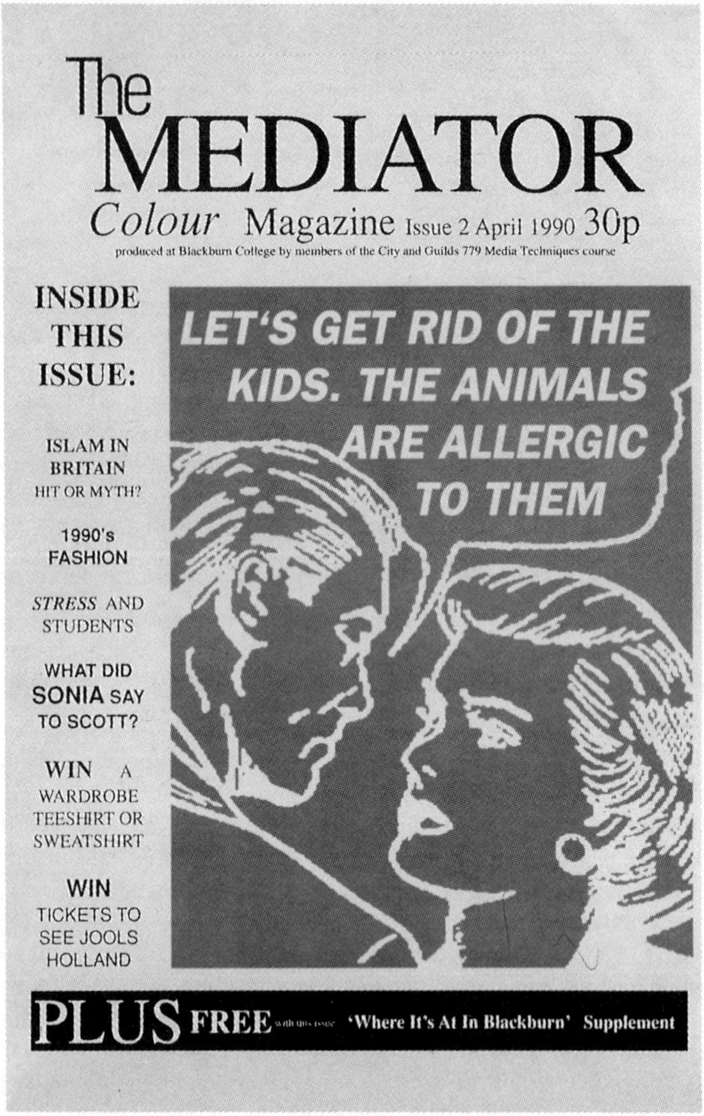

The MEDIATOR

Colour Magazine Issue 2 April 1990 30p

produced at Blackburn College by members of the City and Guilds 779 Media Techniques course

INSIDE THIS ISSUE:

ISLAM IN BRITAIN
HIT OR MYTH?

1990's FASHION

STRESS AND STUDENTS

WHAT DID SONIA SAY TO SCOTT?

WIN A WARDROBE TEESHIRT OR SWEATSHIRT

WIN TICKETS TO SEE JOOLS HOLLAND

LET'S GET RID OF THE KIDS. THE ANIMALS ARE ALLERGIC TO THEM

PLUS FREE 'Where It's At In Blackburn' Supplement

Figure 6.5 Reduced cover of Mediator newspaper published at Blackburn College using DTP

In-House Materials

The production of professional training notes, policy documents, mission statements, minutes, agenda and other materials for internal consumption in your organisation is almost certain to improve the self-image of your colleagues and, as a result, the prestige of your organisation. Naturally this is subject to the content being as professional as the presentation.

Presentation Materials

Making a business presentation with the aid of DTP programmes and other associated software can be highly effective. In the process of persuasion visual impact is often of prime importance. Specialised presentation software in which you can create a colour slideshow and structure ideas, like Aldus Persuasion or Microsoft Powerpoint, contain DTP elements which allow you to print out the text and images showing on the screen of your computer. (If you're using the right equipment the computer is the same one you use for your desktop publishing.)

There are hardware and software packages available which can turn your computer slideshow into 35 millimetre colour slides for photo-projection, and with a colour laserprinter you can produce colour print versions too. This extension of DTP into presentation work, including photographic publishing, is developing fast. Once you have mastered the basics of monochrome desktop publishing you might well find the potential of visual presentation work an invigorating challenge.

7 DESIGNING YOUR PUBLICATIONS

The key to successful document design is to combine the text, headlines, rules and graphics in a such a way that there are no obstacles to your reader taking in the information you are presenting. An overdesigned page can produce a visual barrier to readers who don't share the designer's taste. An underdesigned page can leave errors which get in the way of the message or leave readers wondering why they are bothering to read it. That said there is probably no such thing as the perfect page. The most we can strive for is the effective page. Take a look at a range of newspaper pages, catalogues, leaflets, advertisements and invoice forms and keep the ones you like in a handy file. Ask other people you know to bring you their choices. Although there is a vast range of printed material to choose from you will find that this random sample of pieces chosen as 'effective' share certain characteristics which you will need to absorb into your own work. Some of these characteristics are discussed in the sections which follow.

Ten Common Design Errors And How To Avoid Them

1 'I'm not paying for blank paper – fill those spaces up'

Every designer of newspaper display advertisements has a number of clients who have given this instruction at some time, and the advertisements produced for them are often a mass of boxes and lines filling every millimetre of space inside the text area. To do this well is very difficult. At best the advertisement will appear strident (because the text has been made as large as possible within each type area), and at worst it will look cheap (because a lot will have been made of a little, with the same prominence given to minor items as major ones).

There are certain types of retail trade in which this sort of appearance may be an accurate reflection of the business, and thus this 'bargain

Figure 7.1 The 'no white space' style of display advertisement

basement' style may be appropriate. For most purposes you will create a better impression on your reader with a use of white space which allows the eye to be drawn to important parts of the message.

2 'That area of text will fill the space if you make it a fatter typeface'

True, it will fill the space if you change the type specification. of a short column of Times 12 point into Helvetica. But if your page is unbalanced as a result don't be surprised. When you change from one font to another you change the shape and proportion of the white space you can see on the page when you look at it rather than read it. If the changed type specification hits the eye harder than you intended, swap it back and use one point size increments to make the text fit the column, or increase the leading step by step. If the worst comes to the worst, add some more words to the text. Any of these will alter the visual effect less than changing the font.

True, it will fill the space if you change the type spec. of a short column of Times 12 pt into Helvetica. But if your page is unbalanced as a result don't be surprised. When you change from one font to another you change the shape and proportion of the white space you can see on the page when you look at it rather than read it. If the changed type spec. hits the eye harder than you intended, swap it back and use one point size increments to make the text fit the column, or increase the leading step by step. If the worst comes to the worst, add some more words to the text. Any of these will alter the visual effect less than changing the font.

Figure 7.2 Changing the font helps to fill the space available

True, it will fill the space if you change the type spec. of a short column of Times 12 pt into Helvetica. But if your page is unbalanced as a result don't be surprised. When you change from one font to another you change the shape and proportion of the white space you can see on the page when you look at it rather than read it. If the changed type spec. hits the eye harder than you intended, swap it back and use one point size increments to make the text fit the column, or increase the leading step by step. If the worst comes to the worst, add some more words to the text. Any of these will alter the visual effect less than changing the font.

Figure 7.3 Increasing the leading helps to fill the space available, and may make the text easier to read

There are basic rules about line length which you ought to observe. Two and half times the height of the font is the minimum line length, eight times the height the maximum line length. In practice this means put an average of twelve words on a line and your readers will be happy. Use short line lengths with large body text and they won't be.

3 'Always show the reader the picture first and that means put it in the top left corner'

This advice was dinned into me by the designer in the first publicity department where I worked. It's not a universal rule. You only have to look at any newspaper front page to see that. But it was the house rule for the sort of internal publicity leaflet the department produced. With such little leeway for changes to a layout, one wonders why there was a need for a designer in the first place, but it does illustrate the importance of setting house style rules.

Your basic decisions about what belongs where on the page can be taken from a variety of sources. Better to base those decisions on observation of good practice than make random decisions.

4 'Let's have a bit of variety. Reverse out that headline. Great'

The truth of the matter is that reversing out, so that white text appears in a black box, is a matter not to be taken lightly. It's not a good idea to reverse out a serif typeface. Serif typefaces, like the one used for the body text of this book, even at quite large sizes, are prone to collect toner (or ink) in the curly bits when they're surrounded by black. Sans serif faces, like the one used for the heading above, fare a lot better, so for this reason alone it's best to specify a face like Helvetica, or, even better, Helvetica Bold to avoid these ink traps.

5 'Let's have a bit of variety. Reverse out that text against a 60% tint. Great'

Now this is really a terrible idea. Under no circumstances should you reverse out smaller type sizes against a tint background. And under no circumstances should you reverse out a serif face, like Times, against

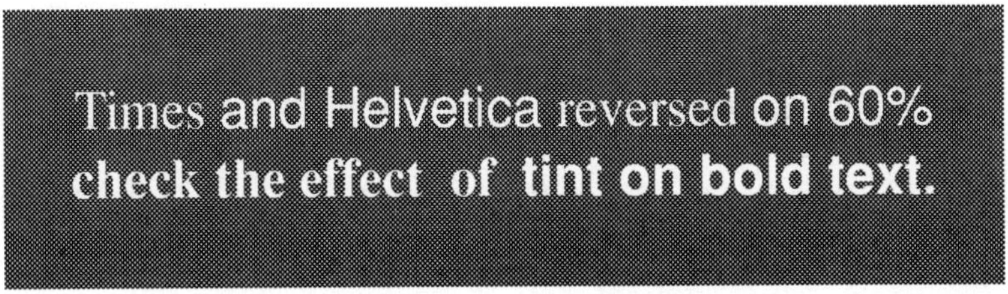

Times and Helvetica reversed on 60%
check the effect of tint on bold text.

Figure 7.4 Text reversed on 60% tint

any sort of tint. The reason for this is that the dots which make up the tint interfere with the edges of the letterforms, making them appear jagged. One way round this is to specify outline type, so that you get a black border around each letter. But this is not always an attractive solution. You may get away with the effect with a sans serif typeface, like Helvetica.

6 'We're going to use tints of varying intensities across the corner of each page in our PageMaker publication to help the reader know where each section starts and finishes'

Not a good idea. Even long-time PageMaker users say: 'Let the printer put the shades in'. Shades which look fine on-screen can vanish when you output them on a Linotronic (in the case of 10%) or look woolly (at 60%) in the final printed version. Your printer will charge you a little extra to put them in manually, but it's as well to let him do so. At least you'll get accurate shades.

7 'That heading's too small. At 24 points it's only twice as large as the body text. Lets make it 40 point and it'll fill that space up'

Everyone has to face the temptation of upping the font size of a headline to make it fit the space available. But we all need to temper our enthusiasm for the ease with which desktop publishing allows us to do this. There is a relationship between the size of the body text and the size of the headline which it is necessary to preserve to produce effective layouts. To ensure your page is easy on the eye of even the most average reader you should be able to divide the larger sizes by the smallest and come up with a number which is at best a whole number, and at least proportional. Thus if your body text is 10 point, 20, 30, 40, 60 point headings are desirable. With 12 point, 24 , 36 , 48 and 60 point headings are desirable and so on. If you do deviate from this rule, make it only by halves. Thus with 10 point body text, you could try, as well as the whole multipliers, 25, 35 or 45 pt and so on.

8 'Headlines in DTP documents take care of themselves. Just specify the type size and font'

Not true. Any line of text above 18 point needs kerning. The space between the letters in a headline can always be improved, which is why you need a package which includes accurate kerning for optimal spacing.

COMPENSATION RULING SOON

Figure 7.5 This text has not been kerned

COMPENSATION RULING SOON

Figure 7.6 This text has been tightly kerned. Compare especially the spaces around the Os

9 'Everybody uses block paragraph style in business nowadays. Just leave your paragraphs as a carriage return'

Another idea which is best ignored. Good DTP programs allow you to specify paragraph styles so they automatically space, and if you wish, indent on the page in response to the carriage return in the word processing text. Paragraph spaces should be more than a single line of type deep, which is what a single carriage return gives you. Set the specifications for your own paragraph spacing in the appropriate style menu.

10 'Don't bother changing the type specifications to get italic, just do Command-Shift-I'

If your font list includes oblique versions and bold versions of a particular font, say Helvetica or Times, specify them. For various reasons making a font bold or italic is likely to give poorer results than specifying the font with those characteristics built into it. On your font list these will be described, for example, as 'B Helvetica Bold' or 'I Times Italic'. Use them for optimum effect. But if you don't have these font versions in your system, just keep on with specifying from the type style list.

▩ Ten technical points you need to know _____

1 'When should I use a serif as opposed to a sans serif typeface?'

In general your body text is better in a serif typeface, because people find it easier to read. The 'curly bits' allow expert readers to scan the

Figure 7.7 Sans serif R is Helvetica – serif R is Times

text more quickly, and less expert readers to decipher meaning more easily.

If you look at national newpapers, for example, you will see that headlines and cross headings are very often specified in sans serif type. Some newspapers do have a house style based on serif face headlines. It is very rare though for body text to be in a sans serif typeface, except in short bursts. When it is, it is almost invariably on the sort of page where many small areas of text are boxed-up, like a diary or entertainment feature page. On such a page, where the visual appearance of variety is deliberately sought, a mixture of type styles can be employed. Otherwise, stick to serif for body text, sans serif for headlines.

2 'This page has a lot of text on it. For variety can I split it up into areas of different typefaces?' _____

Yes, but there are limits if you are to avoid confusing your readers. In general three different typefaces and five different sizes on a page are the most that even a broadsheet newspaper would use for editorial material. Some typefaces do not go together well. The more you use, the more likely it is they will clash.

A random range of sizes in a range of typefaces will certainly make your reader uneasy. In general readers are used to first paragraphs being in larger body text as well as bold. Cross headings, and introductory subheadings can be in different typefaces, as can captions, which are traditionally done in italic or oblique faces. For advertisements and leaflets, where effect often depends on typesetting technique, you could use whatever typefaces you think are necessary, and treat the typography in quite an extravagant manner. But for larger, text-based layouts, limit your faces and sizes.

3 'I want this layout to have authority. What face should I use?'

Most readers perceive a serif typeface as more authoritative. They associate typefaces like Times with established values and tradition. Sans serif faces are generally perceived as modern and efficient.

The TIMES

Figure 7.8 The serif face Times is seen as authoritative and traditional

The TIMES

Figure 7.9 The sans serif face Helvetica is seen as modern and efficient

4 'The round-cornered box looks great, don't you think?' __

If you want your artwork to remind people of highway traffic signs, carry on with the round cornered boxes. Some DTP programs offer you the facility to specify the radius of the corners on such boxes. In general the bigger the radius the softer the effect of the box. There are occasions when you might want to soften an effect with round cornered boxes, but usually you would be better advised to use a square cornered box. Round ones make your page look weak.

5 'Those columns aren't level at the top and bottom. Never mind, nobody will notice '_____

This is just not true. Take great care to align the type if you use columns in your layout. Readers are used to text lining-up accurately on a page. Use the guides you can pull from the margins of the desktop in most DTP programmes to check the horizontal alignment of columns of text – they do not print. Or you can draw your own line with the line tool and delete it when you've finished.

6 'For added emphasis in a line of type use the underline instruction under text style specifications '_____

No, don't. In almost all cases using the underline option will produce a line which cuts the descenders of your text, and leaves too small a space below the baseline. It produces much better results to underline separately, using the line drawing tool. Then you can adjust the position of the line to make the spacing as effective as possible.

The quick brown fox jumped over the lazy dogs.

The quick brown fox jumped over the lazy dogs.

Figure 7.10 The underline option is above, the second line of text is plain with an added rule. Judge for yourself which one you prefer

7 'My local newspaper uses really heavy black rules. They must be at least ten points wide sometimes. Is this a good style pointer for me to copy?' _____

Rules need to be kept thin. The reason your local paper does this is because it a thin day for news, and a fat black box (*a*) makes a story seem more dramatic without having to rewrite the text and (*b*) replaces a column of text, thus saving journalists work when the deadline is coming up. There's every reason to believe that a one point rule is adequate in almost all circumstances as a divider on the page.

8 'This diagram on the layout is just sitting there in a white space. Is that good or bad?' _____

In general it's good. You could draw a box round it to tighten up the space it occupies, but more often than not an uneven white space around an irregular object will heighten the reader's interest and draw more attention to the artwork than if its crammed into a small space surrounded by text.

For line drawings, diagrams and bit map images in general it's better to present them in a definite white space. But for photographs it is often best to surround them with a reference box. This is simply because people are used to seeing photographs as snapshots. They carry with them an expectation that a photograph is bounded by two lines, that is the edge of the image plus the edge of the paper. This isn't literally the case, of course, and many designers do not like to see reference lines on photographs on a page. But if you examine many magazines you will see plenty of examples of single and double boxes around photographs.

9 'To get top quality artwork into my layouts I want to buy a scanner' _____

Certainly, get one if you have lots of memory in your computer system and a need for lots and lots of illustrations. The quality of line art, in technical illustrations for example, can be exemplary from a scanner. If your need is for photographic quality images you might be best not buying a scanner. Save on capital costs and pay your printing company to strip in the photographs in the space on the layout.

Although scanning technology is improving all the time, the best facilities cost a lot of money. Unless you are entirely geared up to do photo-reprographics, rely on your printer for photographic illustrations.

10 'Should I squeeze the leading to get all this text onto one page?'

That's not entirely what leading is for. There are proportions in the space between lines that need to be preserved. Indeed compared to the automatic setting of leading, most text looks better with extra leading rather than less. If you have to reduce the leading very considerably to make text fit into a given space, you might be better advised to go down a point size and enlarge the leading to fit the space if necessary.

That's not entirely what leading is for. There are proportions in the space between lines that need to be preserved. Indeed compared to the automatic setting of leading, most text looks better with extra leading rather than less. If you have to reduce the leading very considerably to make text fit into a given space, you might be better advised to go down a point size and enlarge the leading to fit the space if necessary.

That's not entirely what leading is for. There are proportions in the space between lines that need to be preserved. Indeed compared to the automatic setting of leading, most text looks better with extra leading rather than less. If you have to reduce the leading very considerably to make text fit into a given space, you might be better advised to go down a point size and enlarge the leading to fit the space if necessary.

Figure 7.11 At the top is a column of text in 11 point on 13 point leading. Below is the same text in 12 point on 11 point leading. Judge for yourself which one is most readable, given that they occupy the same amount of space

Ten Communication Factors which Every DTP User Needs To Know

1 European readers scan a page from top left to bottom right. The elements on your page need to create a flow which readers can scan in this way.

2 Non-European readers may scan from right to left or from top right to bottom left depending on their language backgrounds. If you're intent on marketing outside Western Europe or if substantial ethnic minorities make up part of your clientele, it is worth considering multi-language desktop publishing. Cyrillic, Urdu, Arabic, or the Japanese Kanji fonts, as well as fonts for a variety of other non-European languages, can be obtained from specialist suppliers.

3 Headline writing is not a task to be taken lightly. As a rough guide a good headline will have five words in it and provide enough information to tempt the reader to read on. Less than five words is likely to produce a dull title.

4 It is more effective to draw attention to a word or phrase in an area of body text by emboldening it. Underlining and italicising are both possible, but less effective.

5 A strong alternative to presenting lists is • bullet points, rather than Arabic or Roman numerals or letters. Bullet point lists are not hierarchical, and give equal weight to each entry.

6 The key to writing readable copy is to cut out any words which do not (substantially) affect the meaning of the sentence in question. You need never employ 'however', 'so', 'as' and other connectors. 'He told me that he was leaving' means exactly the same as 'He told me he was leaving'.

7 Readers will accept column layout which runs either over and under *or* left and right when the text separates around another element on the page. But whichever you choose should be continued on each page of your layout. Mixing the way columns separate will not only confuse but also antagonise your readers.

Indeed there is some evidence that readers prefer single column layout in all formats other than newspapers and magazines.

8 Copy which includes quotes from people who are clearly identified in the text is more attractive to readers than copy which claims 'some people say…' or has no quotes at all. This variety of sources approach to writing copy seems to reassure readers of the 'real' nature of the story being told.

9 Reader resistance to commercial personalised mail is directly proportional to the amount of such mail received. Whilst computer mailing lists make such personalised items possible, the reader-novelty factor is diminishing sharply.

10 Quality in communication is a product of audience-appropriate text, design and materials, not cost.

8 PRINTING YOUR PUBLICATIONS

■ Commercial And In-House Printing _____

DTP systems are mainly used in commercial publishing and printing and in-house publishing.

In the former, computer systems drive sophisticated output devices, for example Linotronic typesetters, which have the capability of printing at up to 2,450 dots per inch(dpi) resolution. Such photosetting equipment produces very high quality print. If you have your own DTP system, and a local printer or Linotronic Bureau has compatible equipment, you can get your work printed to very high standards direct from the file on your disk.

In the latter, laserprinters provide 300 dpi resolution output for those documents which do not need to be produced in the highest quality or

In-house		Commercial
reports	magazines	
sales leaflets	books	
posters	newspapers	
advertisements	catalogues	
newsletters	handbooks	
forms	instruction manuals	
business reports	guidebooks	
presentation documents	calendars	
training notes	art printing	
instructional material	advertisements	
policy documents	directories	

Figure 8.1 Formats

the greatest number. The chart in Figure 7.1 shows the main formats characteristically produced by in-house and commercial publishing.

The crucial distinctions between the two sorts of publishing are evident from the comparisons in this chart. Firstly the in-house desk top publisher is not concerned with the very large print runs associated with commercial publishing. Secondly, the high quality of printing associated with commercial publishing is not a requirement of in-house publishing. There is a crossover area where your DTP system can produce artwork which then goes to the commercial printer for better quality finish or large print runs. Many DTP users discover that their relationship with local printers develops very quickly. In order to get the best service and results possible, you need to converse with the printer on an informed basis. The terminology of printing is an essential part of desktop publishing.

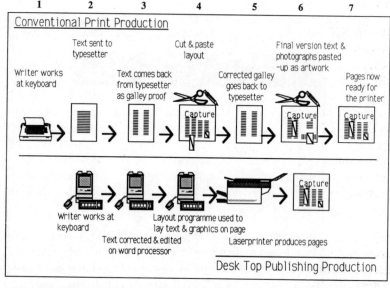

Figure 8.2 The differences between traditional and DTP printing

There are significant differences between traditional printing processes and desktop publishing. The stages involved have been reduced and control over them has been handed to the people who have access to DTP equipment. This can be a mixed blessing, since the expertise your company needs to develop was once the preserve of craftsmen. With DTP in your office and at the printing company, however, you can have the best of both worlds. You can reduce the preparation time and use the printer's expertise on the finished product.

Many printers have taken up DTP technology enthusiastically and use their systems to replace all the traditional stages from point 2 to point 5 in the upper part of the diagram. As a DTP user your crossover point with your printer is at stage 3. For large print runs and high definition printing the disk with your documents stored on it goes to the printer for output on a photosetting machine instead of a laserprinter.

9 LEARNING LAYOUT SKILLS

▮ Introduction ─────────────────────

If you have never used a DTP package, and you can persuade your local dealer to allow you an hour of practice time, the exercise that follows will show you the basic processes involved in working up a page layout. If you have already bought your new system, try this exercise out as your first step.

The exercise introduces you to a range of layout processes using PageMaker as the DTP vehicle. If you follow the text for the project, work it up on-screen and then develop your own version, you'll quickly grasp DTP ways of doing things. Because of the flexibility of PageMaker each user develops a personal style. Combinations of short cuts, of which there are many, can speed up your work. You will soon adopt the particular short cuts that you need for your work.

If you meet a term or an instruction you don't understand, check the DTP glossary for key terms. Once you're used to the language of DTP you'll also be used to DTP processes.

▮ Make your own certificate ────────────

You will practise launching PageMaker, setting up the page, specifying and positioning text, using rules, boxes and circles and specifying them, moving about the page and saving your work.

The formal layout of the average certificate is the secret of its power to impress. The elements are limited: a title, a logo or symbol, an introduction, the name of the recipient and the signature of the issuer. These elements are often framed in boxes or borders. Certificates are more usually printed landscape; that is, wide rather than high.

Open PageMaker, under the File pull down Menu click on New and in the dialogue box that arrives on screen set up a single page document, A4 wide. Click on OK.

If the page that arrives on the screen shows column guides, go to Options on the menu bar and click and hold. Drag down to Column Guides and in the resulting dialogue box click on the number of columns box and enter 1. If that box is reversed out (that is white lettering on a black background) simply type in the figure 1.

Click on OK, or hit the return key, and your page will show with no column guides. You want your certificate to print in the centre of the paper, so click on the File Menu and go to Page Set-up. In the resulting dialogue box, check that all four margins are set to the same value. You'll have considerably more white space on this job than on most. Set the margins to 20mm if they are not already an equal value. In either case click on OK. This value will allow you to use the margin lines on the page as the marker for your main box.

Normally you are best advised to keyboard your text in a word processing program and import the text to PageMaker. In this case the wordcount is so low that you have nothing to gain by doing this. So click on the Text Tool in the PageMaker toolbox and click the I beam inside the margin lines on the page to launch the insertion point.

Normally it will appear against the left-hand margin. If your default setting is other than Align Left it could appear centred on the page, or on the right-hand margin.

It doesn't matter with this project. Wherever the insertion point (also called the cursor) appears, begin entering the text in bold below or your own similar version.

Short cut: If you are in reduced view and cannot see the text you are typing press Option/Command and click the mouse button with the cursor on the page to get full view. This also works in reverse.

Certificate (*hit carriage return*)*

The Mallard School of Ducking, Diving and DTP (*hit carriage return*)*

Certifies that (*hit carriage return*)*

is a registered trained person in the main stream (*hit carriage return*)*

Signed

Secretary General

* this is an instruction to you, not a piece of text.

The page will now look something like this:

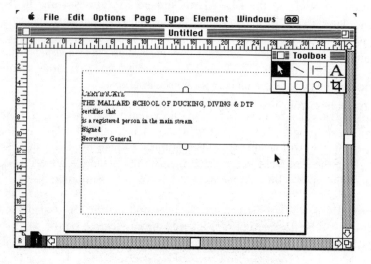

Screen Dump 9.1

You now need to make your certificate look as official and 'real' as possible. For conservative seriousness let's specify Times as the typeface.

Short cut: Triple click the cursor between any two letters and the whole of the text should become highlighted. The text should be reversed out white on black if this is the case.

Take the cursor to the Type Menu at the head of your screen. The cursor will change into an arrow.

Click on Type and a column of items will appear. Click on type, and go to the first entry, 'font'. This produces a list of the available typefaces. If your default setting is Times, it will already be selected, indicated by a tick, in which case leave it as Times. If any other typeface name is indicated, run down the list of fonts that appears when you click on the arrow until Times is highlighted and let go. This will change the font on your screen to Times.

Now click and hold the mouse with the pointer on Type again. This time go to the second entry on the menu, Size. Let go of the mouse button on 12 point.

Click OK and you will be back at the page in no time with your text in 12pt Times. Your text should still be highlighted. Your page will now look like this:

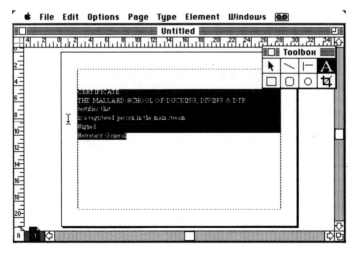

Screen Dump 9.2

Don't click on the page yet. If you do the highlighting will disappear and you'll have to highlight it again. Instead go direct to the Type Menu again, click and go to Type Alignment. Let go on the entry 'Centre'.

Short cut: Instead of going to the Type Menu at the last stage you can press Shift/Command/C to centre the type.

At this point, and at least once every twenty minutes after this, you must save your work. To do this, go to the File Menu and go down to Save As... When you let go a dialogue box will appear. Give your work a recognisable name. It is important that you should always be able to recognise a file name when you need to get back to the work. So call this 'Certificate' perhaps with the date expressed briefly, as in 12/12/91.

Check that your work is to be saved to the floppy drive rather than the hard disk by clicking on the Drive button. In general it is better to save to a floppy than on the hard disk. Click OK and you'll be back on your page.

Next, click anywhere except in the highlighted area and the text will no longer be highlighted. Go to the pointer tool in the toolbox and click on it. The cursor will now be replaced by the pointer. Take the pointer to the middle of the text area and without moving the mouse when you do so, click once.

This reveals the 'roller blinds' which mark the top and bottom of the text block. If there is a downward pointing arrow in the flag in the middle of the bottom roller blind, click inside the flag and hold, pulling it downwards and let go. If the whole of the text is present there will be no mark in the flag. On early versions, a hache symbol (#) indicates the end of the text.

Now check that the ends of the roller blinds, which are marked with a tiny box we'll call 'ears', are lined up on each of the left and right margins. Put the pointer in the text block and click, hold and wait until a large cross with points on it appears.

When it does, slide the text block upwards, still holding the mouse button down, until the top line of the text block is about 10mm below the margin. When it is, let go of the mouse button, after checking that the roller blinds are still lined-up with the left and right margins.

Go to Save As, and save again. This time you'll get an extra dialogue box which will ask you whether you want to replace the existing 'Certificate' as shown in the screen dump below. Click on the Yes button.

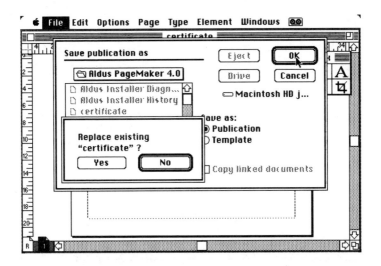

Screen Dump 9.3

This updates the saved version to incorporate the changes you've made. You can simply click on 'Save', but this often produces much bigger files that use a great deal more memory than is really necessary.

Now you've performed your save, click on the text tool in the toolbox.

Take the cursor to the word 'Certificate' and click at the end of the word, drawing the cursor along the length of the word until it, and only it, is highlighted. Go to the Type Menu and select Type Specs again. Enter 102pt in the Type Size box. Click on Bold in the style option and hit the return key. Check the result for size. Then highlight 'The Mallard School of Ducking, Diving and DTP' and specify it to fit on a single line. Try 24pt bold.

Leave the lines 'Certifies that' and 'is a registered trained person' in 12 point plain text, but make the 'Signed' and 'Secretary General' 12pt bold.

Short cut: To make selected text bold, press Shift-Command-B on the keyboard.

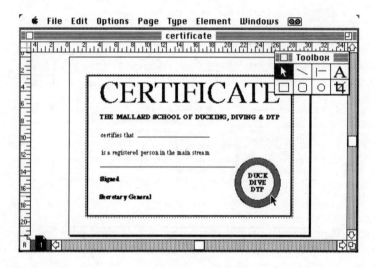

Screen Dump 9.4

Insert the cursor at the front end of the last line and do two or three carriage returns to create a space. Do the same between the other lines to space out the text on the page. If you do too many, the delete key will get rid of them a line at a time.

Now click on the line tool (the one with two lines at right angles, not the diagonal one). Move the cross hairs to the point just below and to the right of the 't' of 'that' in the line 'Certifies that'.

Click and hold the mouse button and at the same time press the Shift key. This guarantees that the line stays straight, and saves your eyesight in checking the fact.

The line is finished when you let go of the mouse button. But by going to the pointer you can select the line again and resize it whenever you wish by clicking on the ear at one end of the line and dragging it.

The whole line can be adjusted for position by clicking and holding on the line itself. This generates the cross with arrows on it that we've mentioned before.

Remember if you click and hold and move the pointer before this cross appears you won't be able to see the line and thus accurate location is difficult. Wait for the cross to appear when you want to move any item on the page.

Draw a second rule across the page below the 'is a registered trained person in the main stream' line. Adjust it so it is centred between that line of text and the 'Signed' line by using the pointer.

You will often attempt to select a particular item, and find that instead you appear to have selected a different element to the one you intended. This is a consequence of the layered nature of a PageMaker page. Elements are stacked up one on top of another wherever they overlap. Either try and select the item at a point where it does not overlap any other, or, where this is impossible, whatever item is selected instead of the one you intend should be sent to the back of the stack of elements by going to the Edit Menu.

Short cut: Hit Command/B to send a selected item to the back of the stack.

Now select the square box tool in the toolbox and take the crosspiece to the top left-hand corner of the dotted margin line. Click and hold and drag the crosspiece diagonally down and to the right. The box you are drawing will follow the tool for as long as you keep the mouse clicked. The borders of the screen are 'hot'. That means that when you hit them your box automatically carries on growing.

When you see the bottom right-hand corner of the margin line keep the mouse clicked, but stop the crosspiece from moving down and right if your reactions are quick enough. If you've gone too far track the mouse up and left a little until the box corner coincides with the margin corner. Now let go of the mouse, and the eight 'ears' or 'handles' which mark a selected graphic will appear. While these ears are present you can select a range of rule weights under the Line Menu.

If by chance you click before reaching the Line Menu, you will have to select the pointer and click on the box with it to select it again. Click on the Line Menu and pull down to the triple line and let go. Your single line box will become a triple line. This carries a certain weight and authority well suited to a certificate. Do another Save As...

Now you should have an unoccupied space in the bottom right-hand corner of the area within the box, which would be ideal for placing a seal or a logo. Try this simple logo.

In the toolbox select the circle drawing tool. Move the tool to the upper left of the available space, click and drag towards the bottom right. When you let go you will have a roughly circular shape, unless you kept the Shift key pressed, in which case it should be as circular as the tool can manage. When you let go of the mouse button, the eight ears will show on the shape.

Short cut: At this point, with the ears showing on the circle, press Command/C followed by Command/V and an identical circle will appear, usually above and to the left of the first one.

This one will show the ears of a selected object. Press Shift and click and hold in a corner ear, and drag inwards to make the circle one third or so smaller. Let go and put the pointer on the line of the circle itself. Click and hold again and when the cross with arrows appears, move it to the first circle and centre it up inside the original. With the Shift key pressed down click on the original circle, and you can then move both circles together to your chosen location. Click off the two circles, taking care not to select any other element.

Select the outer one and go to the Shades Menu. Click on 40%. The circle will fill with shade, and the other circle will apparently have disappeared. Don't worry. Press Command B while the larger circle is still selected and the inner circle will reappear. Select it with the pointer and go to Shades on the menu bar and click off on White.

You will now have a shaded circle with two lines on the inner and outer edge. Select the Text tool and click underneath the outer box you drew on the certificate. Keyboard in the word 'Duck', specify 14 or 18pt Times bold and with the pointer, click and drag the word into the upper part of the inner circle.

Repeat this process with the words 'Dive' and 'DTP'. Arrange the three separate components inside the circle.

There's your logo. If you want to adjust its position again, you can hold down the shift key while you click with the pointer on each of the five elements that make up the logo. Then, making sure you're not clicking on any ears, click and hold and you can drag all the grouped items into their final resting place. If you do make a mistake, don't panic and don't click on the page. Instead go to the Edit Menu and let go on Undo. The last status of your page will be restored.

Check the position of all the elements in the Actual Size mode, which you select either by doing Command/Option/click or by going to the Page Menu with the pointer. If you are happy that all the elements are aligned accurately, go to Print under the File Menu and run off your proof copy. Check it for accuracy, and if you're happy that it looks right, with white space evenly distributed and the different sized lines of text comfortably spaced, the job is finished.

Close the file by clicking on Close under the File Menu, and open a new page to the same specifications.

This time make your own certificate straight onto the page but click the cursor in a new position for each line of text you write. This will create separate elements for each line, which you can then practise towing into position. Don't forget that the window blinds have ears which you can select and tow to the nearest margin. This will guarantee that when you highlight the text and centre it, the line will be absolutely centred, whatever size and style of text you specify.

See whether you can make your own certificate in less than 20 minutes!

10 BUYING DTP PRODUCTS

■ Finding a supplier

Buyers have a number of choices as to their source. There are computer magazines in which you will find advertisements for mail order companies. You can send off for their advertised equipment and it arrives at your home discounted and sometimes without a great deal of support from the supplier. Then your local computer store may be offering discounts too, and among the stock of games and unbranded disks there may be couple of machines lurking under a poster which says 'desktop publishing special offer'. The official dealers will offer you their respective advice on why their product is the best. But in the end you decide on the relative merits of the source yourself. It is a budgetary and a lifestyle issue as much as anything else.

If you have a lot of time and patience lying around, don't worry about the fact that you can't get support but you can get a big discount. Go mail order. But at least check the specifications and performance of what you're ordering. If what you want is assistance and fast after sales service with some training thrown in as part of the deal, use your official supplier. If you've got a lot of friends with computer experience, especially in DTP, take time to get their views.

You can rent, lease and buy outright in the computer market. There are second-hand machines about, but not very many that are good for DTP and prices seem a bit high in many cases. Much better to go after a discount from an official supplier.

■ The system

A desktop publishing system is a personal computer connected to a full-page or two page monitor, a laser printer, and, if you want to use graphics regularly, a scanner. To make it work you'll need graphics and word processing software, a page make-up program, and the software to drive your scanner. You can buy these items separately from different suppliers or as a package from a single supplier. You cannot avoid making a choice between the major operating systems on the market.

The computer route is either IBM compatible or Apple Macintosh unless you have a great deal of money to invest in a Sun or Apollo workstation. Because of it's ease of use, the Macintosh is often said to be the most productive machine available. The main advantage it has is that programs for it generally work in very similar ways, so that once you have used the Macintosh in one software package, you can easily pick up ways of working in others.

The laserprinter

The laserprinter can come from a variety of sources. Manufacturers of your PC will tell you theirs is the superior one, but there are many others on the market which may suit your computer, so it might pay you to shop around. A direct question, 'Is it compatible with my computer?' should be sufficient to get some promises. Some models come with their own built-in microprocessor and memory units. PostScript printing requires this sort of printer. Others are directly supplied from your computer's memory and microprocessor. They are thus considerably cheaper. However, if you do buy other than a recommended laserprinter, check on the conditions of the guarantee on your computer, and the supplier's service and support arrangements for your laserprinter. Be aware that you will need to replace your toner cartridge regularly, after between two and three thousand pages. Your laserprinter warning light will tell you when that's required.

Some suppliers will refill your existing cartridge at about half the price of a new replacement, although opinion is divided over whether the cartridge mechanism will maintain its performance for two or more cycles. On balance it's probably better to have your own cartridge refilled, rather than inherit one that might have been filled three or four times already.

Printer manufacturers also advise regular changes of the exposure drum, which is the heart of the laserprinter technology. Check the recommended frequency of this replacement before you buy. Prices for drums vary, and they are not cheap. Colour laserprinters are developing fast, and on the higher specification models the results are impressive. If you work a lot in colour they are worth purchasing, but for most purposes a monochrome printer will be more economical and reliable.

The section on printers will give you some technical and performance details about laserprinters and the options available. Printers are discussed in more detail on pages 72–76.

The monitor

You need a large monitor to see your page layouts at full-size. Large monitors always seem to come as optional extras. The advantage is that you will save yourself a great deal of time because small screens mean you spend a lot of time moving the field of vision from one part of your work to another. With an A4-sized screen you'll also avoid eyestrain. If you're likely to do a lot of double-page spreads (that is A3 folded to A4) an A3 monitor would be a distinct advantage. If you are likely to use a lot of photographic content in your page layouts, then you need a greyscale monitor. If you're doing a lot of colour separation work then an A3 colour monitor will cost you rather a lot of money, but you'll need it.

The scanner

There are many makes and models of scanner on the market. Monochrome scanners are sufficient for most users, and they are cheaper now than they've ever been. There are some roller-fed models, which require you to spend time cutting pages out of books, magazines and newspapers to feed into the rollers.

These have been displaced by the user preference for the flat-bed scanner. With this, you place your artwork on a glass plate with a lid, very much like a photocopier, and scan diagrams, sketches, paintings and photographs into digital form in the memory of your computer. The scanner will come with the software you need to get the images onto your screen. If you need photographic quality, then you should get a scanner which can reproduce good quality grey scales.

Technically that means you need to check that you're getting an 8-bit scanner not a 4-bit scanner. Whilst the latter can reproduce photographs, you're limited to 256 shades of grey which might reduce the clarity of the photographic image when you print it.

A good scanner can also save you a lot of keyboarding time with Optical Character Recognition. This facility allows you to scan-in typewritten and other text which then becomes a word processing document which you can edit on the screen. Check that the scanner you are considering offers good OCR standards. Some don't.

If you do not consider expense a problem, or if you're working in full colour printing a lot of the time, you might want to consider buying a colour scanner. The cost of these is reducing, but they are still expensive. For occasional users the best course is probably to find a local bureau with a colour scanner and rent some time on it. Scanners are discussed in more detail on pages 76–78.

The software

The software route has more choices. Some DTP packages are less impressive than others, some rather complicated for beginners. For most purposes the choice is between Aldus PageMaker (for both IBM or Macintosh) and Ventura Publisher (for IBM).

PageMaker is the programme most used by DTP practitioners. It is an 'integrating' package which allows you to bring-in materials from other programmes. After a little practice you'll be able to locate and import onto a page in PageMaker any text or graphic file in the memory of your computer.

Why A Laserprinter Is A Good Investment

Although there are some options open to you, desktop publishing essentially requires you to buy and use a page printer. Realistically that means a laserprinter. Desktop publishing first became possible in the 1970s when Xerox produced the Alto workstation which was built around a laserprinter and the ability to produced printed materials from a single desk, albeit a large one.

1985 marked the real start of DTP, the year when Aldus introduced the PageMaker program for the Apple Macintosh. The DTP market gathered momentum quickly, and a great deal of development has gone into the printing and publishing aspects of personal computer use. All of it depends on laserprinter technology for its effect.

Laserprinters are built with connections for a range of personal computers, but not all of them can connect with all PCs. In general they fall into either the IBM-compatible group, or the Macintosh group, with a number of machines which emulate other sorts of computers and printers in between.

You can connect a laserprinter to one single machine, or to several machines by coaxial or twin cabling. Occasionally one user may have to wait a short while to gain access to the printer on a network, but this is usually only a few seconds. Some computer makes or models may need all their memory resources to control the printing process. Others may allow you to continue work while the printing goes on 'in the background'. Like most computer facilities, this background printing mode is likely to cost you more money for more memory. But it is worth asking your dealer when you buy a machine whether you can have this facility if your time and productivity are very important to you.

In terms of the technology the laserprinter ranks as a recent invention. The first laser was demonstrated in 1960. It produced a light beam composed of 'coherent' light. Other light sources spread their light in all directions, but laser light travels in a single direction and can be aimed with great precision.

There are many types of laser technology. Carbon dioxide lasers are widely used in industry where powerful cutting tools are needed, and in medicine. Excimer lasers are used where heat generation is not required, especially in measurement. Solid state lasers are used in welding, ionic lasers in research, helium/neon lasers in discotheques and barcode scanners, and laser diodes in communication and desktop publishing.

A laserprinter is an intelligent photocopier. Technologically speaking, they are both 'page printers'. It is what we call 'the front end' that separates the two. When you place a master sheet on the screen of the photocopier the light beam reflects the light and dark areas onto the exposure drum. This is the 'physical front end'. But with a laserprinter your computer sends the image in digital form to the laserprinter memory, where the laserprinter is programmed to produce on the exposure drum, line by line, the pixels (short for 'picture cells', widely known as 'dots') which make up your document. This is the 'electronic front end'.

From this point, the photocopier and the laserprinter work virtually identically. The negatively charged exposure drum is written on with the laser and wherever the laser touches, the negative charge goes to earth. It is these discharged areas where the toner collects. Both printers take a sheet of positively charged paper and pass it over the drum, where the toner is concentrated on the black shapes of the original. Particles of toner are attracted to the surface of the paper and are melted to the surface when the paper passes between the press and heat roller.

The quality of print you get from a modern laserprinter is excellent. Standard resolution is 300x300 pixels per square inch, sufficient for all but very fine printing work. A full A4 page coming out of your laser printer may have had up to eight million pixels built-up on the drum during the print preparation. You will soon learn to expect complex pages to take a few more seconds to print out, compared with a simple letter heading.

Other printers

Laserprinters can produce several pages per minute, and are useful for producing complex layouts of text and images. Other sorts of printers have their strengths, and you may need to consider what uses your printer will be asked to perform, and at what speed you wish to produce as well as at what quality. Other sorts of printers are given the generic name of 'serial printers', because they produce the page by large numbers of line-by-line passes. They are divided into impact printers and non-impact printers.

Line printers

These are widely employed in computer centres. They come with various drive systems, but in all of them, single characters are punched through a coloured cloth ribbon onto paper at very high speed. Up to 2000 lines per minute can be continuously achieved, at the expense of a great deal of noise. Impact printers are kept inside sound-proofed canopies for very good reasons.

Dot matrix printers

These are commonly produced with 9, 18, 24 or even 48-pin print-heads. In general the more pins, the more definition in print. Some dot matrix machines are noisier than others, so test the one you're offered. Soundproof hoods can easily be obtained, but it is a nuisance constantly to have to raise and lower the hood of a frequently used machine. Some dot matrix printers can reach speeds of close to 1000 characters per second, others are slower. In general, the better the print quality you ask the printer to produce, the slower it will run. Most allow you to specify draft quality (very ragged but very quick), faster and best (the slowest).

In draft quality you will not get the page as you designed it. In faster and best you will.

Daisy wheel and golf ball printers

These are much slower, often as little as 50cps. In general the product you get will be standard size body text which looks very like typewriter output. This is because both these sort of printers are borrowed from typewriter technology. If all you want to produce is pages of typewritten text, with perhaps bold and underline as the only style options and one column or two the only text layout option, this type of printer may be a good investment. You cannot produce page layouts with it.

Inkjet and thermal printers _____

These are becoming very sophisticated, and if you have a need to produce single master pages in colour, then either of these might be useful. They are both non-impact printers, becaue the print mechanism does not touch the paper directly. The inkjet has a printing head with 9 or 18 nozzles from which tiny ink drops of different colours are shot onto the paper with considerable force.

Used for black print only speeds are slow, perhaps up to 540 cps. Output of colour illustrations is very slow, but the printers are almost silent in operation.

Thermal printers have up to 40 heating elements which pick up colour particles from a number of coloured tapes and burn them into the paper. They run even more slowly than inkjet printers, at anything from 20 to 130 cps, and they require special thermal tapes and paper which can be expensive. However, in their favour is the silence of their operation.

Other Varieties of Page Printers_____

Most other page printers vary from the laserprinter only in the way in which the information is transferred to the exposure drum. You may see LED (Light Emitting Diodes) printers, or LCS (Liquid Crystal Shutter) printers, or even magnetic or ionic printers. Only the first offers improvements in definition, commonly 400 dpi. The others offer 300 dpi or less. There will no doubt be improvements in these as well as laserprinter technology.

▉ Do You Really Need A Scanner? _____

This is the section that the ladies and gentlemen at Abaton, Agfa and Neotech will be turning to first and so let us now praise the technology of the scanner. National newspapers are now produced with scanned rather than screened images, and occasionally you can see the moiré or tartan pattern that demonstrates the scanned image has not been reproduced at the right definition level, like the example below:

Figure 10.1 The patterned effect caused by resizing a photograph
TIFF file

Scanners are getting to be very sophisticated devices. Earlier forms worked at low resolutions. Now 400 dpi is common. Similarly scanners used to come with 4 bits of information per pixel, now they can have up to 24. This allows the scanner to reproduce a wider range of greys, usually expressed as grey scale. A 4-bit scanner will give you 16 greys, an 8-bit scanner will give you 256 which is what you need for halftoning. A 24-bit scanner conveys enough information to scan colour images.

There is a wide range of prices on scanners. The most expensive is between four and five times the cost of the cheapest. In general the cheapest are usually less sensitive, but the price difference between a 4-bit and an 8-bit scanner is often fairly small. It is probably best to avoid a 4-bit scanner unless you are going to be using it mostly for line art. If you want to scan photographs you need a grey scale scanner, and that usually means 8-bit.

For all-electronic publishing a scanner is a must. You can crop, resize and treat images in a paint or photo programme like Superpaint or Digital Darkroom, load them onto your page in a page layout programme, and print them out on your laserprinter or Linotronic.

But in the end the question that arises is this. The alternative is to strip in the illustrations manually at the final stage before printing. Now the higher the level of printing you are going for, the better your graphics will reproduce, especially the grey scale ones like photographs.

If you're planning to photocopy a few items at a time from your laserprinter output, then a digitised photograph you scanned into the page will actually reproduce better than a stripped-in photograph. If you are outputting your artwork to a Linotronic, and assuming you have better than a 4-bit scanner, there should be very few problems with reproducing photographs. Otherwise, you might get better results from the traditional stripping-in of illustrations by the printer. It costs you a little extra on your print bill, but if the results are better, why not?

Essentially this is the decision you have to make. If your work is going to contain a lot of photographs in a range of sizes within a complex document, then you can save a lot of money on your printing bill by investing in a high definition scanner. Equally, if you are not likely to use many photographs, but are likely to include a large number of drawings, plans or other artwork, then any scanner is a good investment. But, if your publications are most likely to be text with occasional photographs or line art, get the photographs stripped in by the printer, and don't buy a scanner.

■ Services You May Need To Buy In _____

There are two major sorts of services for which a desktop publisher might discover a need. The first is pre-production and research services, including electronic mail. The second is production services in terms of printing.

Communications _____

There are a number of highly developed information services that you might need in order to perform research or simply send and receive messages. Whilst this need is not peculiar to desktop publishers, the electronic information systems like Telecom Gold and CIX can be a vital part of the publishing process. Using an E-mail system means that people can get their copy to you within minutes (when systems are running properly), and you won't need to keyboard their contributions as you would if the copy was faxed or phoned to you.

You can download files from the system and save them in your own computer, then import them into your document and specify the type and layout styles. If you are likely to include copy written by people outside your base office then an E-mail subscription is well worth considering. You will need a Communications package of software such as Vicom, a modem which runs at 1200 baud or more (300 baud modems are cheaper but much slower), and the fee for your annual subscription to the E-mail service. The advantage is that you can also send copy to other people who are subscribers, and you will find other uses for the communications software and modem. What you cannot yet (if ever) do is to send formatted copy. Only ASCII files can be sent into communications systems. There is no way that style instructions like those on a finished layout can be transferred into E-mail systems.

Linotronic Bureaux

The second area of production services is much more clearly a distinct part of publishing. There will be in your locality at least one Linotronic bureau. Here your documents, laid out in your chosen DTP programme, are taken on disk (or sent through the phone line using your communications package) to be processed on a Linotronic typesetter. The output comes in the form of high-definition bromides from which the printing plates will be made at your printers. More complex documents can take longer to typeset, and you should be prepared to be charged on the time it takes to set your pages.

Graphics Studios

You may find that your graphic skills need bolstering by local graphic artists, many of whom are themselves working on computers these days. Find out which studios are capable of producing work electronically, and buy in their designs already on disk, so that their files can be entered straight into your work, or kept as whole pieces of work for later laserprinting or Linotronic output. Rates will vary according to the type and style of work you want them to do. In general you will save money by getting their work in on disk, rather than contracting out an entire print job.

CASE STUDIES

Robert Maybin runs a busy small town estate agency and an auctioneers business. He has used computers since the middle eighties for commercial and financial operations in his business.

Maybin says he thinks he was ahead of his time in 1986 when he installed an Apple Macintosh computer with a modem for on line information services. 'Everyone's doing it now' he says. He subscribed to Prestel for City news and information. Since the Big Bang in the City an insurance company has been providing him with financial services on an Olivetti which is a stand alone machine. Information is brought in on disk by the insurance company's area information manager for regular monthly updates.

On his own PCs he keeps his client databases and accounts. 'I'm used to computers' he says, sitting in front of a big Apricot with its hard disk whirring. 'This one went down a few weeks ago. The hard disk crashed and we lost every single piece of information in the business. Everything had to be keyboarded back in. It was my fault. I knew I should be backing-up the work, but you just get used to the reliability of the machine. Then the crash. Now we back-up our work every day.'

Desktop publishing is a new venture for Maybin's company. He saw an advertisement in a PC magazine for the budget package *Timeworks Publisher* by GST Software. He bought it from the local distributor who's name and number he obtained from GST with a single phone call.

'Price was the main factor in the choice' he says, 'along with the claimed ease of use'. The system comes with three typefaces to drive a dot matrix printer. There are two faces called respectively Serif and Sans which look very much like a dot matrix version of a typewriter. The third face is Zapf Dingbats, the symbols and patterns collection. None of them print very impressively on the dot matrix printer currently connected to the Apricot.

Extra typefaces for *Timeworks Publisher* are available at extra cost, and Maybin is looking into getting hold of them. He has already invested in a laserprinter, but that is not yet connected. When it is, he will need the fonts to drive it. As a minimum he should get Helvetica and Times to produce faces his customers will recognise as 'professional'. He could also consider buying Univers which is currently undergoing a revival, and a showier font for display work, perhaps Bodoni.

Timeworks Publisher is good value for beginners in DTP. On-screen you can see half an A4 page. You draw a text box, a little like Ready Set Go, and go to the Place Story instruction, where you locate the text you've prepared in your word processing package. With the text flowed onto the page layout, you can add boxes and other graphic elements as easily as with any programme costing four times as much. You can style the text, and a big bonus is the presence of a stylesheet feature in which you can set up the preferred type styles simply and quickly for a single document or as a permanent template feature.

Maybin says after three days, and without the aid of a mouse, he was producing his property leaflets on the system. 'The manual is very clear, and although having to move the cursor from the keyboard is time consuming, I'm pleased how quickly I've learned. I'm already thinking of ways to make it work for us.'

This is a permanent feature of any DTP package worth its purchase price. If you can learn it quickly and produce your documents satisfactorily, you will begin to think of new applications in which you can employ your new skills. Maybin is already considering using his software to help him produce his press advertisements, posters for the business and regular newsletters.

'The newsletter is something I'm keen to develop for the estate agency' he says. 'We have between fifty and sixty clients at any one time. That's too small to do what the big corporate estate agencies do and produce commercially printed newspaper-style publications. I'm thinking about an A3 photocopy folded to four sides of A4. We could update the details to keep track of new properties and sales, laserprint the master and produce copies as and when we need the stock. People have come to expect agencies to produce a master list of properties. By using even a low cost system like this, we can meet their expectations without generating big costs.'

DTP is an ideal route forward for a business where low print runs and ease of update are important factors. And with recent improvements in photocopier technology, printing jobs which would otherwise not be cost effective can be tackled very simply. Lay out your information and print the pages on your laserprinter. Photocopy them a few at a time. Reprint them as stocks run low, and in a few minutes a week you can keep up with demand in a way which would be impossible without DTP.

Maybin is currently producing his property detail leaflets partly by DTP and partly by having them typed. The two are at present virtually indistinguishable. Without a range of fonts he is limited to producing dot matrix versions of of the typewritten leaflet. As his expertise develops and he has a range of laserprinter fonts he expects to develop a new leaflet, possibly by using a standard template with styled headings and improved layout.

Already he is planning to use on-demand publishing to pare costs further. At present his sixty or so properties each have a stock of leaflets. People can browse through them and take them away if they are interested. He intends to pilot a scheme in which a single leaflet is left on display. A notice asking customers to request their own copy will be on show. Using readymade templates a laser copy, perhaps including scanned-in artwork and photographs, could be available in seconds. The bonus here could be improved company contact with prospective buyers. Time will tell whether the plan is an improvement on the current browsing system.

What is interesting is that a new DTP user like Maybin already sees the potential of his system. His route consisted of adding a low cost package to his existing personal computer system. The overheads are small, and the probability of improved efficiency is high. What is his next project? 'I'm just going down the road to buy a mouse' said the desktop publishing estate agent.

The Accountant and His Publication _____

Mike Wills is a chartered accountant and a partner in a northern accountancy company. He was formerly a tax inspector. Each year he produces an overnight publication explaining the budget changes to PF Pierce and Company clients. He is interested in finding out how this job could be done using DTP techniques.

The Story of the Budget Booklet _____

The Budget booklet is one of only a handful of guides produced by provincial companies for their local clients. Partner Mike Wills travels to the headquarters of the Inland Revenue on Budget Day. Press releases are made available at Somerset House at the moment the Chancellor sits after his speech in the Commons. Wills has tried having the information delivered by facsimile transmission. But there are usually between two and three hundred pages which take a lot of hours to receive. He's tried flying and driving to collect the information but says the train is fastest, and he still has time to write his notes in longhand on the journey back to the north.

He says: 'Round about nine o'clock that night we have a meeting with 15 or 20 of our senior staff. The pensions and insurance specialists, computer people, other senior staff and the partners. Members take the sections of my notes that seem to fit their specialism and write a commentary which they check with me. This takes until midnight as a rule.'.

Wills then edits the resulting hand written scripts and ends up with 10 or 15 sets of text which he organises into a draft page structure. He says: 'It's a cut and paste method, but without the paste. It's a basic job in which I Sellotape or staple the edited scripts onto A3 pages which represent the content of the eventual A4 pages.'.

Soon after midnight the resulting commentary pages are taken to a local printer to be computer typeset. From about 10.30 pm the lists of the Chancellor's changes have already been taken for typesetting. The cover has been printed several days in advance, with design work by a local graphics company. Wills says: 'Before the event I write some sort of commentary for the cover which is ready about a week before the budget. I live in fear of having thousands of these covers printed and then the Chancellor resigning. But that hasn't happened yet.'.

Staff have spent several hours carrying pages of text to the printer about two miles away to be typeset. By about 3.00 am the galleys have been proofed and last-minute style changes incorporated. The plates are made and the print run of about 2000 begins. By 6.30 am the junior members of staff not involved in the writing phase arrive to distribute the booklet by hand. Local branches of banks and building societies, professionals and the company's clients have a copy on the premises the morning after Budget Day.

Mike Wills says: 'We have some fairly sophisticated computer equipment networked throughout the office which we didn't have last time. For the next booklet we're looking at how we can use computer-based methods.'.

The Budget Booklet using DTP Processes

Mike Wills needs a portable computer for the return journey from London. It doesn't have to be an expensive one. As long as it can export word processing files to the computers in the network at his office any model will do.

Using his portable, Wills can keyboard the information he selects from the Inland Revenue documents instead of writing by hand. There is a new generation of portable computers which will recognise handwritten messages. They are not yet a replacement for keyboard machines.

Once the primary files have been created, they can be downloaded onto the office network. Given a trouble-free journey Wills would be back in the office at about 7.00 pm on budget day. Downloading the files will take only a few minutes. Hard copies could be printed in the following few minutes so that his writing team can discuss their contributions by about 7.20 pm.

At the computers in their respective offices the writers will find, given adequate keyboard skills, that writing time is less than doing the same job by hand. Text can be cut, revised or extended in seconds without impairing its legibility. Wills can visit each writer and discuss the text as they work, or he can wait to see their contributions on screen via the network in his own office.

Within an hour he will have text to subedit into its final form. By 9.00 pm the lists of budget changes will be complete, the bulk of the descriptive text will be finalised, and it will be time to create a master disk and a back-up version. At this stage it only takes a few minutes to print out the text so that he can edit on hard copy.

Each file will be saved with a clear prearranged title. Wills may already have had time to draw up a preliminary layout. A set of thumbnail sketches would suffice, using the agreed titles to indicate the pages on which each topic will appear.

He now has a choice to work out with their printer. He can deliver the text on disk and the thumbnail layouts for the page layout to be done at the printers. The alternative is to use the same page layout programme the printer uses and lay out the pages in-house. This alternative requires a member of staff with at least minimum proficiency levels on the page layout programme and familiarity with layout conventions. In future this expertise will probably develop in-house. At first it is probably best to let the printer do the final layout.

Allowing for any extra writing or rewriting, the text on a set of files on disk, with its back-up copy, should be ready to go to the printer already proofed and subedited, by 10.00 pm. Given explicit and accurate instructions on the layout sheets, carefully integrated with the titles on each separate piece of text , the printer will be able to produce precisely the result the company requires.

By 10.30 pm the staff of PF Pierce and Company can be back in the bosom of their families. Mike Wills no longer needs to check the galleys at 3.00 am, because he did that in the office from the hard copy and amended the disk version accordingly. The entire task can be completed in about half the time it took previously.

And the cover can be printed in the same print run, with a commentary prepared after the budget, not a week before, simply by adding new text to an existing page design direct from disk. Then Mike Wills' fear that a Chancellor will resign before Budget Day can be laid to rest, courtesy of desktop publishing.

The Teacher, His Work and His Pupils

John Flanagan is a graphic designer and he lectures in a further education college. He has been using desktop publishing in education for three years.

'I trained as a designer' says John Flanagan. 'So I'm comfortable with the world of printing and publishing. Having said that when I first came across desktop publishing equipment I felt an excitement about the prospects it opened up for my design work and my teaching.'

In Flanagan's case that excitement led him to buy a top of the range Macintosh computer which he uses at home, and at work he uses both an IBM network and a range of Macintosh machines with design students. His recently acquired computer skills have changed the way he works. He says: 'I place great value on students working as professionally as possible. Their design course must develop them personally and get them ready to earn a living in the business. When I began preparing materials using DTP the effect was immediate. Instead of handwritten or typewritten sheets I could provide them with professional looking designed pages. That alone sets their targets higher. If you're a designer everything you produce is a test of your design skills. I produce assignment materials, briefs, assessment records and a range of course materials and administration documents using DTP. It takes less time than doing it by hand, it makes me feel more organised and I suspect it impresses students and colleagues alike.'.

Flanagan points out that a large part of teaching is delivering the learning experience. He believes that students learn in a more coherent way using computers in design. 'There are some students who will never develop the basic skills of using a graphics package, even though they're good designers. There's a distinct lack of hand to eye coordination in a few people. They normally elect to rely on traditional methods of putting marks on paper. That's often a good thing anyway. There are some jobs that will always be done better with paper and a pen. A few people just can't work out what the equipment is doing. One key here is to not worry about what's happening, but just to go after the results. Familiarity rather than understanding is the key thing with design work on computers. There's another group who seem to click with the computer straight away. Often on the first day. They see all sorts of ways of using the facilities as soon as they find them. That leaves the majority who can use the computer capably, and use it sensibly but economically. There's very little spare time on our computers.'

If delivering the course experience is the teacher's task, how has DTP affected Flanagan's performance? He points out that because DTP requires the creation of systems within which publishing takes place he has adopted a more structured approach to his work. 'When you save a document you've created you have a permanent magnetic record of that file. I back-up each file and keep a catalogue of disks at work and at home. The technology means I work more at home than I used to, but for some reason that's a pleasure rather than a burden. I'm much clearer now about what's involved in my job. I feel more organised without being swamped by paper work.'

Course administration requires the production of class lists, schemes of work, student records, agenda and minutes for course meetings and reports. Flanagan uses DTP for all these functions. Many of his forms are templates which are filled in by hand. What they all have in common is that they are legible and nice to look at without being fancy. With his publications he has created an identity for the courses he leads. The impression of cohesion and organisation is deliberate.

'Too much organisation of students can be counter-educational' he says. 'What I can organise is the course feel and philosophy, and present that to the college authorities and the external assessment body in an organised and structured way.'

It may be that Flanagan is a gifted teacher who would do all this without the aid of DTP. But he says otherwise. 'The Macintosh has made me organise myself. Because I have so many files on my machine there seem to be fewer gaps and crises. There's very little that happens without me already being aware of an impending need for information or action. I think DTP allows me to organise and initiate quicker and more positively.'

Flanagan's DTP output in his own design work is impressive. He is especially skilled in typography and illustration, using programmes like Aldus Freehand for typography and Image Studio for illustration. He exports files from these programmes into PageMaker for layout. Working like this he has produced multi-page colour printed publications for a nationally known theatre company, a large number of one-off design jobs and a range of corporate identities for a variety of commercial companies.

He explains the DTP effect as follows: 'It allows me to combine my existing skills and abilities with a technology which allows me to be productive. Before DTP I would have had to use other people's skills because they had the technology and I didn't. All I needed was one computer and the right software. Now I can work right up to the final output stage myself. Then I pop down to our local image setting bureau and off come the bromides ready to make the plates for printing.'.

The Student and His Efforts to Learn _____

Zaffer Khan is a nineteen year old student studying for his A levels. His ambition is to be editor of a national newspaper before he is thirty years old. And he is prepared to start his own paper if an existing title doesn't recognise his worth.

When Zaffer Khan was seventeen he approached one of his teachers to request training in desktop publishing. He had twice edited a school newspaper using typewriters, scissors and paste. He says: 'I knew there was a better way than enthusiasm and hit or miss techniques. I just had a feeling, because I didn't know much about it, that DTP was the answer.'.

Khan had plenty of experience of using IBM PCs for word processing, but none on Apple Macintosh. After fifteen sessions of two hours training a week on the Media Techniques course at his local college he began the layout for his first publication using DTP equipment. *The Mediator Magazine* was a 36 page A4 publication financed by advertising, written by a team of twenty people, laid out by Khan with guidance from his tutor. He says: 'It was printed in three colours and had a print run of a thousand. The magazine was widely regarded as the best student publication anyone who bought it had ever seen. We set out to do a serious product, a sort of *Student Statesman*.'.

Khan says: 'It aroused a lot of interest that we could produce work to a professional-looking standard like that. The writing was good, but the presentation was so good that it seemed to make the writing even better. I was very pleased with the result.'.

Now he had tested his DTP abilities, Zaffer Khan's ambitions grew. During the next summer he went out selling advertising space for his next editorial project. The *Son of Mediator* was to be a full-colour popular tabloid newspaper aimed at the 17 to 19 student market which had been lukewarm about buying the serious magazine.

'The paper is to be printed on the presses of the local evening newspaper,' says Khan. 'We do the page layouts in PageMaker with stories written by students on the journalism course. The *Evening Telegraph* are doing the colour separations for the pages with colour photographs, but we are doing everything else. We couldn't do any of this without the DTP equipment.'

In Khan's case an interest in a career in newspapers led him to learn the skills of DTP. Those skills led him further down the road to understanding production processes than could have been possible without DTP. He says: 'I wasn't the first editor of *The Mediator*. The girl who did that first edition did such a good job that I could go round to advertisers and persuade them easily by showing the previous product that it was worth spending money with us. That was done using DTP. The results speak for themselves. I've learned about the commercial side of newspaper production. Without DTP I couldn't have the same confidence in our ability to get professional-enough results to please advertisers, so I wouldn't have done so much commercially. I've learned about working to deadlines and getting organised to meet them. And I've learned a lot about how not to issue orders and getting on with people. All of that is based on access to DTP equipment. I'm also a lot more confident in my other studies as a result of my experience.'

Many newspapers are produced on equipment which works very much like the equipment Khan's team used for their publications. His skills will be transferable wherever he works. His ambition is to edit a national newspaper before he is thirty. Without DTP that ambition might be dismissed as adolescent dreaming. But anyone who has seen Khan performing with DTP knows he has a better chance than almost anyone else of his age.

Khan sums up his philosophy with these words: 'Do you want to advertise your book in the next edition of my paper?'.

▉ The On-demand Administrator

Jackie Gill is a twenty-two year old Public Media graduate of Leeds University. She joined the Macintosh DTP environment at The Press Bureau from a job in computing. Jackie's role in administation and business development supports the work of four journalists, and they are all intent on cutting the paper out of electronic publishing.

Jackie Gill works for The Press Bureau, the Blackburn computer news agency. Although much of her work consists of word processing to produce standard pages of news copy, she uses desktop publishing techniques for a range of administration and communications tasks.

Working on Apple Macintosh computers, Jackie uses MacWrite or Word 4 to produce text for letters. The text is checked for spelling and punctuation in the word processing package. When it is corrected she calls up a pre-designed PageMaker letter heading page. Using the 'Place' command, she puts the text onto the page, adjusts it to fit the space available, and goes to 'Print' on the Laserwriter.

Seconds later her letter rolls out of the printer and she sends it out. She says: 'When I came here I had not used page layout programmes. But after a few days I was confident to do it. The advantage is that we don't have to keep stocking up on pre-printed stationery. I don't know whether it's cheaper to do it this way, but it does mean that you can print a letter page anytime. It's a form of on-demand publishing I suppose.'.

In addition to creating letters by DTP, Jackie also does all her invoicing on the page layout programme. The entries are pre-set, and she simply updates the record details and amounts for each client's invoice. She says: 'There are accounts packages on the market that

The Press Bureau Limited
Registered Office
7 Simmons Street Business Centre
BLACKBURN BB2 1AX
Contact The Press Bureau
Telephone 0254-62087
Facsimile 0254-662624
Electronic Mail boxes CIX - tpbur
(Compulink Information Exchange)
Registered in England
No.2526357

Figure 11.1 The Press Bureau logo and letterhead,
produced on DTP

generate invoices for you, but we use the standard company logo on a PageMaker document and print them off either singly or as a series of pages. It doesn't take a lot of time, and the advantage is that I didn't have to learn any new procedures.'

Electronic publishing doesn't have to mean hard copies, that is, print on paper, says Jackie: 'Pages that need to be faxed can be downloaded from the laserprinted page. That's the way we do it at the moment. There are plans to introduce a fax modem. That means we will be able to set up the message on-screen. Then with the computer linked to the phone line we can download the laid out page as a Huffman file. The whole message is digital and electronic all the way then. Cutting out the printing section of desktop publishing means less wear and tear on the laserprinter and no paper costs.'

Although fax modem technology is not cheap, the facility to be able to save on running costs is considerable. All-in-one fax modems are the more expensive alternative. A cheaper option is the fax card, which PC users can have installed quite cheaply. This allows the computer to drive a fast modem. The time it takes to route a message from the computer screen to its destination can be considerably speeded up.

Not only are the physical steps involved in producing hard print eliminated, but the speed of transmission compared with a conventional fax machine can produce cost savings. The 9600 Baud standard of the most recent fax transmission equipment, compared with the 1200 Baud standard of most office fax machines, mean that messages can be transmitted much more quickly, even allowing for error checking. So direct fax modem publishing can produce substantial savings on telecommunication costs.

The link between fax technology and computers is giving rise to new electronic publishing opportunities and systems. The Tex Fax system offered by International Textiles Benjamin Dent in London uses desktop publishing techniques to store pages of information created in PageMaker in a computer hub.

Subscribers get a faxed list of categories and contents on a regular basis. They call in by telephone. A voice system in a choice of languages asks them to list the pages they require and reacts to the spoken instructions.

Callers then replace their handset and switch the fax machine to manual receive, and the pages are printed on the facsimile receiver. When a caller has a fax modem, the pages are stored in the computer and can be printed out at higher resolution on the laserprinter.

The system is a clever combination of technologies which allows access to a computer database by people without computers. Its novelty, for the system is very recent, lies in seeing the potential of common office equipment as a means of publishing. Electronic publishing and the electronic distribution of information are merging.

Jackie Gill is confident that in the coming months her output will be increasingly electronic. The company she works for is highly computerised and relies heavily on communications in getting information to newspapers and magazines around the world. Jackie says: 'When we're sending a three page fax of a news story to several titles in Australia or Japan, cost is critical. Our existing BT fax machine is very good, but if we're running a fax modem at our end and the receiver is on a fax modem running at the same speed I'm sure we can save on the phone bill.'.

The Press Bureau staff say they could not operate their business without a computer which can easily handle graphics, word processing, desktop publishing and communications. Their chosen route is Apple Macintosh which, they say, cuts down training time. They are also happy with the number of applications which they can switch between quickly and easily. If the range of publications in which their work appears is anything to judge by, the Press Bureau's electronic publishing skills have made them highly productive. They're banking that increased investment in communications equipment will increase the profitability of their desktop publishing operations.

GLOSSARY 1

A List Of The Words You May Need In Dealing With Computer Sales People And Learning About Desktop Publishing.

alignment – the placing and shape of text relative to the margins of a page (see centred, range left, range right, justified and textwrap).

alley – the space between two columns of text.

anti-aliasing – the process of smoothing out the jagged edges of bit-map lettering.

ASCII – the code in which text-only files are stored. It stands for American Standard Code for Information Interchange. They store text information only in relation to position on the page, not information about fonts and styles.

Autoflow – the fastest way of placing text in Pagemaker. With autoflow switched on your text 'places itself' across as many pages as it takes to exhaust the file. Stop it by clicking the mouse.

bit-map – representations of lettering or graphics made up from pixels, the square dots which make-up the image on your computer screen. They print jagged edges on lettering and 'dotty' images.

bleed-off – any artwork or tint that runs off the edge of a page, usually achieved by printing on oversize paper and cropping down to size.

body text – the main text on your page, sometimes called running text. It is usually set in a point-size between 8 and 12 in continuous paragraphs and/or columns.

border – white space, lines or decorative graphics which define the frame of the printed area, either around a particular element like a graphic or the entire page.

bounding box – this can be briefly seen in PageMaker when you click and drag the cursor/text tool from left to right on the page. This action creates margins within which you keyboard or place the type.

bullets – dots used to denote items on a list (called up by Control-Shift-8 on a PC and Option 8 on a Mac).

caption – text which accompanies a photograph or other graphic element, ideally it should not repeat information in the illustration, but add to it or complement it.

centred – type which is aligned down the centre axis of a column or page, giving both ragged left and right margins.

clip art – non-copyright illustrations you can use without further payment once you've bought either the books or the computer disks they come in. Occasionally you can put clip art to good use.

clipboard – the temporary storeplace for information you have cut out of a document. It enables you to restore the original if you change your mind. The next cut will replace the previous one on the clipboard, so don't delay too long if you want to restore a cut.

column guides – vertical rulers on a PageMaker page which form left and right margins for typed or placed text. They do not print. You can move them manually by clicking and dragging. You specify the number you want to use at the Column guides entry under the Options Menu.

column rules – fine lines separating columns of text.

crop – to trim a graphic in PageMaker to fit a given space by 'cutting' part of it away. Also the physical trimming of photographs and paper.

crop marks – right-angle lines which mark where the page is to be trimmed once printed. You select the crop marks option in the PageMaker print dialogue box if you want to print them.

cropping tool – the bottom right-hand symbol in the PageMaker toolbox which allows you to trim graphics. When you crop a graphic it can always be uncropped later with the same tool.

crossbar – the shape taken-up by the pointer when you select a drawing tool in PageMaker.

cursor – widely-used term for what some manufacturers call the insertion point, the vertical flashing bar which shows where text can be keyboarded-in, or where text or graphics can be placed in PageMaker.

default – preset values or options which the program uses until you over-ride them with your own specifications.

deselect – a mouseclick on a menu item previously selected switches it off. This is deselecting.

dialogue box – the boxes which appear on screen at key times during operations either because you have selected a particular operation which requires you to input details of what options and vaues you want (for example when you call up Type Specs) or because the computer is telling you something is going well or badly.

digitize – the process of turning line and tone art into digital dots to store in your computer's memory.

display type – large typesizes, usually emboldened, used for posters, headlines and display advertisements.

double-sided – printing on both sides of each sheet of paper. PageMaker's Page Setup box allows you to specify single-sided (where the margin is on the left-hand side of each page in the European language versions), or double-sided (alternate left and right margins), usually used in conjunction with facing pages (in which the same story goes over both, giving a **double page spread**).

download – the term used to describe the process by which fonts not normally resident in the memory of a laserprinter are sent from your computer to the printer. An unusual font may need to be downloaded each time you use it, but will stay in the printer memory until you switch off the printer.

downloadable fonts – commercially available typefaces you can install in your DTP system.

drag – to click and hold the mouse as you move the pointer to a new location on the screen.

ellipsis ... – used to indicate an unfinished thought or sentence, or a change of direction in an argument, or to indicate part of an utterance has been cut. Many editors believe three dots is the most you should ever use. Indeed you create an ellipsis of the regulation three dots in many word processing and DTP programs by hitting 'Option-semicolon' like the ellipsis here …

em dash – a dash as many points long as the typeface size you're using. Thus an em dash in 12 point Times is 12 points long.

em space – a space the same point size as the type you're using. In PageMaker an em space is created by 'Command-Shift-m'

EPSF – Encapsulated PostScript Files are in a format that allows you to print line art with smooth lines and edges as well as see and resize graphics on screen. Such images can only be printed on PostScript laserprinters.

en dash – a dash half the size of an em dash, obtained in many word processing packages and in PageMaker by pressing 'Option -'.

en space – a space half as wide as an em space. In Pagemaker 'Command-Shift-n' will produce an en space.

face – the general term for discussing or describing typefaces like Times or Helvetica Narrow. Viz. 'Nice face, shame about the serifs'.

fill – the name given to the shades and patterns used inside boxes or other shapes on the page. PageMaker fills are filed under the Shades Menu. Paint and draw programmes offer a variety of fills, and you can devise your own in some.

fixed space – spaces inserted between characters to spread out a line to fill the available space. Each font and size reacts to a different degree of fixed space. Press Option-Space bar on Macintosh and Ctrl-Space bar on PCs with the cursor between the letters you want to s p a c e o u t.

Some printers have an intense dislike of intrusive letter-spacing. They're probably right, but see *kerning*.

flush – aligned, as in flush left. More usually referred to as *range*.

folio – page number.

font – in printing, font has always meant one typeface in one size; for example: '10 point Helvetica Light'. In desktop publishing many people use 'font' as though it means the same as 'face' – the entire family of letter forms. In fact this is not a correct useage, as any printer will tell you.

format – the shape, style, appearance and treatment of a publication (or an event, television programme ,etc.). In DTP, format includes issues of presentation like size, type of paper, colour of inks; editorial design issues, like headline styles and text column widths; and straight editorial issues like 'Is it a newspaper?', 'If so tabloid or broadsheet?' and so on. Format is collectively the editorial decisions you make about everything except the content of what you publish.

formatted text – text you have saved with specifications to control paragraphs and type sizes and styles in a word processing program or page layout program.

for position only – indication to the printer that there is an illustration to be stripped in at this point on your layout, where you leave a box with FPO written in it, or paste-in a sketch or photocopy of the real artwork.

galley proof – in traditional printing, type was arranged on a metal tray called the galley, and a proof copy of the text was pulled off to enable proofing to take place. DTP retains the term only for the rare occasions when you want to produce text in columns before proof reading the page layout. Most DTP users proof from their page layouts.

Gothic typefaces – serif faces, often with heavy adornment.

grabber – the friendly hand which appears on a Macintosh screen when you press the Option key and on a PC when you press Alt and then click the mouse. Whatever tool you were using in PageMaker becomes a hand which moves the work in whichever direction you drag. It is much quicker and easier than scrolling around, and essential to use the feature when you're working an a small screen.

graphic boundary – an on-screen dotted line around a graphic in PageMaker which dictates how close text can come to the image. The distance is adjustable via the 'standoff' distance in the textwrap feature under the Option Menu.

greeking – replacement of small sizes of text with grey bars which indicate the general size and spacing of lines instead of unreadable detail at fit-in-window screen sizes. The facility speeds up screen redraw. Print designers use the same word to describe mock-ups of their layouts with Latin text used to concentrate attention on layout rather than content.

grid – on-screen vertical and horizontal lines to aid placing elements on a layout.

guides – moveable dotted on-screen lines you can pull out from the margins in PageMaker to assist in placing elements accurately.

gutter – the space between two facing pages. The space between two columns of text, sometimes referred to as the gutter, is more accurately referred to as the *alley*.

hairline rule – a very thin line on a layout. In general they are difficult to reproduce except at very high resolutions. Even 0.5 em rules sometimes print patchily. Most DTP users keep to minimum 1 em rules.

halftone – a representation of a continuously toned photograph with graded dots which appear to be varying grey tones when printed. Originally known as screening, the process involved photographs of artwork being taken through a fine cloth screen. Putting a photograph through a scanner is a form of halftoning.

handles – the eight small rectangles which appear when you highlight a graphic in PageMaker, enabling you to stretch or condense the image. See also *windowshade handles*.

I-beam – the shape you get instead of the pointer when you select the Text tool. The I-beam is clicked in the desired position to create the *cursor*, more properly known as the *insertion point*.

image area – the text and graphics contained within the page margins. Only a handful of elements are placed outside the image area. Page numbers and dates are the usual refugees.

imagesetter – a photo-composing device, like the Linotronic, which outputs very high resolution pages from DTP files.

insertion point – the proper name for what most people call the *cursor.*

inside margin – the space between the bound edge and the text. See *double-sided.*

italic type – letters which slant towards the right, and have been so designed to do. Originally created by Aldus Manutius, patron saint of PageMaker, in 1501. Not the same as *oblique type.*

justified – type that is even on both left and right margins, achieved in Page Maker by adding and subtracting space between words.

kerning – the process of adjusting the space between individual characters in a word, especially in a *headline* , *display type* or in fine typographical work. To decrease in small increments in PageMaker set the cursor in position and press Command-Backspace on the Macintosh and Ctrl-Backspace on a PC. Repeat until the gap is closed sufficiently. To increase the gap press Command-Shift-Backspace on the Mac, Ctrl-Shift-Backspace on the PC. Kerning can make the difference between an average piece of typesetting and an excellent one. See also *em space.*

kicker – a phrase or line before a headline aimed at stimulating the reader's attention.

landscape – the name given to paper laid-out horizontally, that is wider than it is high. Alternative is *portrait.* PageMaker uses the more prosaic High and Wide.

layout – the arrangement of text and graphics on a page.

leading – pronounced as in the metal, lead. The term describes the distance between the *baseline* of one line of text and the next, measured in points. In PageMaker leading is usually automatic at 120% of point size, but you can specify the leading manually during *copy-fitting.*

letterspacing – the amount of white space between one character and the next. In PageMaker you can adjust the letter space through the Spacing dialogue box on the Type Menu.

Linotronic – the phototypesetting device which produces high quality bromides of DTP layouts direct from disk.

manual text flow – the basic way of placing text in PageMaker. The text stops at the end of each column. Click on the roller blind handle at the bottom of the text block. This brings back the text icon, and you can then click at the head of the next column or page. The alternative is to select Autoflow on the Options Menu.

margin guide – the dotted lines that appear on PageMaker documents which you specify in the Page Setup dialogue box. They do not print.

master page – the page icons marked L and R at the bottom left corner of a PageMaker screen. Master page items will appear on every subsequent page and cannot be altered except on the master page.

menu – a list of commands along the top of the screen from which you can select the key operations under the headings File, Edit, Type and so on.

menu bar – the area containing the menu names at the top of the screen.

mini save – an automatic save of a document which PageMaker performs each time you turn pages, change a Page Setup or insert or delete a page.

object-oriented graphics – draw-type graphics made up of a series of mathematically defined curves and lines. Their advantage is that they can be scaled up or down without distortion.

page number marker – automatic page numbering inserted on the master pages in PageMaker. Type 'Page O' followed by Command-Option-P on a Macintosh, Control-Shift-3 on a PC.

page setup – the dialogue box in PageMaker in which you specify the page size, orientation, number and margins for your work.

page view – depending on the size of your screen you can select the view of either Fit-in-Window, 50%, 75%, Actual Size and 200%.

paint-type graphics – *bit-mapped* images made up of *pixels* which can be individually altered on screen.

pasteboard – the area surrounding the page you are working on in your DTP software. In PageMaker you can leave text or graphics on the pasteboard while you change pages.

perpendicular line tool – the tool used to draw vertical and horizontal lines.

PICT format – a file format for saving object-oriented graphics.

pixel – the smallest unit on a computer screen. The number of pixels per inch of the monitor is the measure of screen resolution.

place – the command on PageMaker's File Menu with which you import text and graphics from other application files.

pointer – the arrow shaped icon that moves on the screen when you move the mouse. It changes shape when you select other tools in the *Toolbox*. These other shapes turn back to the pointer tool when you move them off the *pasteboard*.

PostScript – Adobe Systems' page description language used by many laserprinters and typesetters.

printer font – the mathematical code describing the characters in a font which a laserprinter or typesetter uses to print text at the best resolution possible.

proofreading (or simply **proofing**) – the process of checking typeset text and layouts for the accuracy of punctuation, spelling, alignment and other errors an correcting them where necessary. There is a set of standard proofing marks which are available in many reference books.

RAM – Random Access Memory is the part of your computer's memory which deals with storage of information you are currently working on which is lost when you close down before saving.

Revert – the command which allows you to return your work to the state it was in when you last saved.

roller blinds – the horizontal lines with handles in the centre that appear at the top and bottom of a *text block* when it is selected in PageMaker.

ruler guide – the guides you drag in from either the vertical or horizontal rulers on a PageMaker screen to use for allignment of elements. They do not print.

scanner – the hardware device which converts photographs and line art into bit-mapped images which you can save and manipulate to add to your publication electronically.

scrapbook – a feature of Macintosh computers in which you can store text and graphics which can be cut and pasted into applications. The contents are available each time you use your computer.

screen dump – a bitmapped image of the screen you are currently working on created on a Macintosh with Command-Shift-3.

screen font – the screen display of a typeface made up of pixels, which calls up the corresponding printer font during printing.

scroll bars – the grey bars to the right and bottom of a window or palette with which you move horizontally and vertically around the page.

select – the act of clicking on or dragging across text or graphics to make the element active.

selection box – the dotted box which appears when you drag the pointer around several elements at once so the material can be treated as a single unit. Any item not completely enclosed will not be selected.

stacking order – items on a page occupy multi-level layers so that one can be on top of, or below several others. In a complex document the order in which they are stacked is critical. To alter one layer may require dismantling and rebuilding the stack.

standoff – the distance between a graphic and its graphic boundary, governed by the value set in PageMaker Text Wrap dialogue box.

style editor – a feature of DTP programmes which allows you to create a specific style or format in typography or graphics, and store it as a permanent feature of the programme which you can call up at any time with either a keyboard *macro* or a mouse click. This means you never have to do the same thing twice, as long as you store it in the style editor. A valuable productivity feature which must be in your chosen software.

template – a stored layout grid and style sheet saved using the Template option in PageMaker. This facility allows for a particular style to be available for a particular set of documents.

text block – the text on a PageMaker page which when selected has roller blind handles top and bottom.

text tool – the tool marked by the letter A in PageMaker (and a T in some other programmes) which when selected produces the *I-beam* with which the *insertion point* or *cursor* is placed.

TIFF files – a file format used especially for scanned images of bit-mapped grey scale and colour line art or photography. Acronym for Tagged Image File Format.

toolbox – a window containing text and graphic tools.

WYSIWYG – pronounced 'wizzi wig' the acronym for *What You See Is What You Get*. The principle is that what you see on the screen should be what you get in the printed version.

GLOSSARY 2

The following is a list of words which you may need when dealing with printers and getting your DTP layouts ready for printing.

alignment – the placing and shape of text relative to the margins of a page (see *centred*, *range left*, *range right*, *justified* and *textwrap*).

alley – the space between two columns of text.

ascender – the part of a lower case letter that rises above the x height (as in b,t and so on).

baseline – the notional line on which the letters of a line of type sit (except for descenders in letters like g, y and so on, which pass through it).

bleed-off – any artwork or tint that runs off the edge of a page, usually achieved by printing on oversize paper and cropping down to size.

body text – the main text on your page, sometimes called running text. It is usually set in a point-size between 8 and 12 in continuous paragraphs and/or columns.

border – white space, lines or decorative graphics which define the frame of the printed area, either around a particular element like a graphic or the entire page.

bromide – name given to sheets of photographic paper containing text and graphics output from phototypesetting equipment like the *Linotronic*.

bullets – dots used to denote items on a list.

byline – the author's name on a piece of copy.

camera-ready – complete pages, with all text, illustrations and so on in place, ready for the printer to photograph for making printing plates. If you can supply camera-ready artwork you'll save a little money on your printing bill.

caption – text which accompanies a photograph or other graphic element, ideally it should not repeat information in the illustration, but add to it or complement it.

centred – type which is aligned down the centre axis of a column or page, giving ragged left and right margins.

clip art – non-copyright illustrations you can use without further payment once you've bought either the books or the computer disks they come in. Occasionally you can put clip art to good use.

column rules – fine lines separating columns of text.

condensed typeface – narrower than normal variants of typefaces, giving more characters to the line.

copy-fitting – editing and styling text to fit a given space.

counter – the white space inside round letters like e.

crop – to trim photographs and paper to size.

crop marks – right-angle lines which mark where the page is to be trimmed once printed. You select the crop marks option in the PageMaker Print dialogue box if you want to print them.

crossover – type or artwork that crosses the gutter between pages. You need to get your alignment and print areas accurately specified if you want to do this.

descender – the part of letters which passes through the baseline, as in j, p and so on.

display type – large typesizes, usually emboldened, used for posters, headlines and display advertisements.

double-sided – printing on both sides of each sheet of paper, usually used in conjunction with facing pages (in which the same story goes over both, giving a **double page spread**).

dpi – dots per inch, a measure of the resolution at which a *bromide* or other electronic print product is produced. The higher the number the higher the resolution. Professionally the range is from 300 dpi to 2450 dpi.

drop cap – an enlarged initial letter, usually in the opening paragraph, which drops below the first and/or subsequent lines of body text.

ellipsis ... used to indicate an unfinished thought or sentence, or a change of direction in an argument, or to indicate part of an utterance has been cut. Many editors believe three dots is the most you should ever use.

em dash — a dash as many points long as the typeface size you're using. Thus an em dash in 12 point Times is 12 points long.

em space — a space the same point size as the type you're using.

en dash – a dash half the size of an em dash.

en space – a space half as wide as an em space.

face – the general term for discussing or describing typefaces like Times or Helvetica Narrow. Viz. 'Nice face, shame about the serifs'.

fixed space – spaces inserted between characters to spread out a line to fill the available space. Each font and size reacts to a different degree of fixed space. Some printers have an intense dislike of intrusive letter-spacing. They're probably right, but see *kerning*.

flush – aligned, as in flush left. More usually referred to as *range*.

fold marks – part of the layout on camera-ready artwork which indicates a fold-line, for example on a return slip or application form.

folio – page number.

font – in printing, font has always meant one typeface in one size; for example: '10 point Helvetica Light'. In desktop publishing many people use 'font' as though it means the same as 'face' – the entire family of letter forms. In fact this is not a correct usage, as any printer will tell you.

for position only – indication to the printer that there is an illustration to be stripped in at this point on your layout, where you leave a box with FPO written in it, or paste-in a sketch or photocopy of the real artwork.

galley proof – in traditional printing, type was arranged on a metal tray called the galley, and a proof copy of the text was pulled off to enable proofing to take place.

Gothic typefaces – serif faces, often with heavy adornment.

graphics – symbols, charts and graphs, drawings (known as line art) or photographs used to add information or illustration to a *text*.

greeking – on a layout or design, the replacement of small sizes of type with grey bars or Latin text, used to concentrate attention on layout rather than content.

gutter – the white space of paper between two facing pages. The space between two columns of text, sometimes referred to as the gutter, is more accurately referred to as the *alley*.

hairline rule – a very thin line on a layout.

halftone – a representation of a continuously toned photograph with graded dots which appear to be varying grey tones when printed. Originally known as screening, the process involved photographs of artwork being taken through a fine cloth screen. Putting a photograph through a computer-driven scanner is a form of halftoning.

headline – the title of a story or article.

image area – the text and graphics contained within the page margins. Only a handful of elements are placed outside the image area. Page numbers and dates are the usual refugees.

imagesetter – a photocomposing device, like the Linotronic, which outputs very high resolution pages of text and graphics.

inside margin – the space between the bound edge and the text. See *double-sided*.

italic type – letters which slant towards the right, and have been so designed as to use space economically. Not the same as *oblique type*.

justified – type that is even on both left and right margins.

kerning – the process of adjusting the space between individual characters in a word, especially in a *headline, display type* or in fine typographical work.

kicker – a phrase or line before a headline aimed at stimulating the reader's attention.

landscape – the name given to paper laid-out horizontally, that is wider than it is high. Alternative is *portrait*.

layout – the arrangement of text and graphics on a page.

leading – pronounced as in the metal, lead. The term describes the distance between the *baseline* of one line of text and the next, measured in points.

letterspacing – the amount of white space between one character and the next.

Linotronic – tradename for a high quality image-setting device which produces photographic quality *bromides* at resolutions up to 2450 dpi.

logo or logotype – the name or symbol of a company, product or publication designed to produce recognition and recall.

margin – the distance between the edge of the paper and the area occupied by text and graphics.

masthead – details of publisher, issue number, date at the head of a newspaper or magazine cover. Generally now used to include the typographical treatment of the publication name, more correctly called the *nameplate*.

measure – the length of a line of type, traditionally described in picas, but now more likely in ems, millimetres or inches.

modular layout – designed page or spread in which elements are laid out as self-contained units.

monospacing – letterspacing that is the same for every character. Typewriter faces are monospaced. See also *proportional spacing*.

nameplate – the typographical design of the name of a publication.

negative leading – lines of type in which the *leading* is less than the size of the type in order to tighten up a text block, especially on a headline.

oblique type – roman typefaces which are slanted to the right, but otherwise are identical to the upright version. *Italic* faces are designed separately from and different to their roman equivalent.

orphan – an opening line of a paragraph appearing at the foot of a column or page separated from the rest of the paragraph.

outside margin – the margin between the text and the trimmed edge of the page.

paste-up – traditional page layouts are assembled by cutting and pasting *galleys* and *graphics* in place on a piece of artboard with a tissue overlay. Electronic composition has removed the need for most of this paste-up work, but it may still be required for large pieces of work.

pica – a traditional typographic measure in which one pica = 12 points. Roughly equivalent to 1/6".

point – the basic measure of type. 12 points equals one pica. A point is about 1/72".

point size – the distance from the top of the ascender to the bottom of the descender in a font measured in points.

portrait – vertical orientation of a page, that is a layout which is higher than it is wide. See *landscape*.

proofreading (or simply **proofing**) – the process of checking typeset text and layouts for the accuracy of punctuation, spelling, alignment and other errors and correcting them where necessary. There is a set of standard proofing marks which are available in many reference books.

proportional spacing – letterspacing that depends on the size of each individual letter. Thus w takes up more space than t, and the gaps between the letters are proportional to the horizontal scale of each letter. See *monospacing*.

recto – the right-hand page.

registration – the alignment of elements where one or more are to be overprinted, as in colour printing, so the result is accurately aligned.

registration marks – non-printing symbols on layouts which allow accurate alignment of overlays or separations.

resolution – the definition of elements on a computer screen or print output, measured in *dpi*. Print resolution governs the accuracy of lines and curves in type and the clarity of artwork. The more dpi, the higher the definition. Resolution varies from 300dpi for laserprinters to 2540dpi on the *Linotronic* 300.

reverse – white type or rules displayed on a black background.

roman typeface – a typeface with *serifs*.

roman type – vertical type as opposed to *oblique* or *italic*.

rules – lines in typography, measured in points.

running foot – a line of text, perhaps a name or title and page number, which appears at the bottom of each page of a publication to help the reader navigate the document.

running head – as *running foot*, but at the top of the page.

running text – as *body text*.

sans serif – a typeface without finishing strokes at the end of each line in the letterform, thus providing a much more linear outline.

scale – (verb) to calculate the degree of enlargement or reduction on a piece of graphic work to fit the space on the *layout*. For example to reduce from A4 to A5 is 74%.

scanner – a microprocessor-controlled device that reads a photograph or line art and produces a binary file containing a bit-map image. This can be stored and placed on page layouts as an illustration. Many scanners will also read text, so saving time on keyboarding as long as the result is accurate.

screen – a tint or tone of dots in percentages of black or another colour which can be placed behind lettering or art on a layout.

script – any typeface which emulates handwriting.

serif – the straight or curved-edge strokes which finish the vertical and horizontal lines of many letterforms, which are thus called serif typefaces.

set solid – to set text without additional leading, specified, for example, as 72/72.

show through – printing on the reverse of a double-sided page shows through. Care in selecting the paper stock can avoid this.

silhouette – a photograph in which the background has been removed prior to printing.

single-sided – printed materials in which only one side of the paper is printed on.

small caps – a specification to use a smaller size of capital than the rest of the text, usually 70% of normal.

spread – two facing pages in a publication.

stick-up cap – an initial capital letter that stands up above the line of text that follows. Its effect is to draw the reader's eye to the text.

strip in – to assemble all the components of the page to be printed in order to make a printing plate. Electronically laid-out text can have photographic images and tones stripped-in on the bromide.

tabloid – a large format or paper size, most often used for newspapers and newsletters. Tabloid is about half the size of broadsheet, and roughly the same size as A3.

tone – (or **tint**) a percentage shade of black or a colour used as a fill for an area of text or graphic.

trim – cutting the printed pages to size during the binding process of a multi-page document.

verso – the left-hand page.

vignette – a graphic where the shades diminish outwards to white or the colour of the page.

weight – **1** the density of letters, as in the typeface descriptors 'light/ normal/bold'.

      2 the grade of paper used for printing, measured in grams per square metre. 80gsm is relatively transparent, 120gsm relatively opaque.

white space – the areas of the page left free of text or graphics which are vital to getting the message across and which a good designer uses to create deliberate effects.

widow – the last line of a paragraph which runs onto the next column or page. A widow needs to be reunited with its fellow text lines. See also *orphan*.

width – the horizontal measure of a typeface, described as condensed, normal or expanded.

x height – the height of the body of a lower case font, excluding the ascenders and descenders.

Other computing titles available in the **Teach Yourself** series:

Books

WordStar 6 *Alan Winn* (ISBN 0 340 53905 4)
SuperCalc 5 *Diane Saxon* (ISBN 0 340 53906 2)
WordPerfect *Ann Elms & Fenella Deards* (ISBN 0 340 54920 3)
Word 5 *Christopher R. J. Watson* (ISBN 0 340 54919 X)
Lotus 123 *David & Jacky Royall* (ISBN 0 340 55431 2)
dBASE III PLUS *Diane Saxon* (ISBN 0 340 53904 6)
Computers and Their Use *L. R. Carter and E. Huzan*
(ISBN 0 340 35652 9)

Book/disk packs

The book/disk packs contain a copy of the relevant book as shown above, one 5.25" disk and one 3.5" disk. The disks contain the practice material.

WordStar 6 (ISBN 0 340 55428 2)
SuperCalc 5 (ISBN 0 340 55427 4)
WordPerfect (ISBN 0 340 55429 0)
Word 5 (ISBN 0 340 55508 4)
Lotus 123 (ISBN 0 340 55430 4)
dBASE III PLUS (ISBN 0 340 55795 8)

All these titles are available from your bookshop. If you would like more information or a catalogue listing all current Teach Yourself titles, please write to:

The Teach Yourself Department
Hodder & Stoughton Ltd
Mill Road
Dunton Green
Sevenoaks
Kent
TN13 2YA

Computer programming titles available in the **Teach yourself** series:

Computer Graphics *John Lansdown* (ISBN 0 340 40819 7)
Computer Programming in BASIC *L. R. Carter & E. Huzan*
(ISBN 0 340 41765 X)
Computer Programming in COBOL *Melinda Fisher*
(ISBN 0 340 20383 8)
Computer Programming in FORTRAN *A. S. Radford*
(ISBN 0 340 27587 1)
Computer Programming in Pascal *David Lightfoot*
(ISBN 0 340 33728 1)

These titles are available from your bookshop or direct from the
publisher.